they met again on several occasions. One was the Punta del Este Conference at Montevideo, in August of 1961, in the course of which attempts were made at a reconciliation between the U.S. and Cuba, using the presidents of Argentina and Brazil as intermediaries — with disastrous results. Then, in 1963, Ché had Rojo flown up to Cuba and in lengthy discussions revealed his plans and vision for Latin revolution (including the suggestion of harboring Juan Perón in Cuba to use as a threat against the Argentine government). Rojo gives details of Jorge Masetti's little-known insurgency in Argentina — which Guevara conceived and whose unsuccessful example he followed in Bolivia — and he recounts Guevara's trip in 1964 to Moscow and North Africa, the apparent slippage of his authority in Cuba and his break with Castro as read between the lines of correspondence with his mother, and his leaving Cuba in 1965. The narrative follows Guevara to the Congo, where he fought against white mercenaries, and then to Bolivia. The last chapter gives a full account of Ché's unsuccessful efforts to raise the Bolivian peasantry, and of his death at La Higuera.

With its wealth of important disclosures on the life and thought of Ché Guevara, **My Friend Ché** is a singularly valuable document. It is also a moving and immediate portrait of one of the most fascinating political leaders of our day.

My Friend Ché

My Friend Che

RICARDO ROJO

Translated from the Spanish by Julian Casart

THE DIAL PRESS, INC.   NEW YORK, 1968

"We must grow tough,
but without ever losing
our tenderness."

CHÉ GUEVARA, 1967

FOREWORD TO THE AMERICAN EDITION

I began to write this book shortly after Ernesto Guevara's death. In spite of this, I've tried to tell the story dispassionately, in order to give an unbiased appraisal of him and of those who had anything to do with his end, either directly or indirectly. Only I know how difficult this has been for me, at a time when his death seemed as unreal to me as it did to millions of persons all over the world.

The idea of telling in a book my experiences with Guevara during fourteen years of friendship grew out of a circumstance of which I became aware only after his death—I believe I am one of the very few who knew him well both before and after he stepped into history. It was this special position made me decide to write this book, which is not a systematic biography of Ché but a tentative reconstruction of the principal stages of his life, discovering the man who was buried under the myth.

In order to reconstruct my years close to Guevara I had my own notebooks handy, several dozens of them. If they did not serve as my only source, they constituted a documentary substructure, especially when it came to dates and places mentioned, as well as the textual transcriptions of conversations with Guevara and other persons who appear in the story.

I also decided to include a letter to Ché from his mother, since I had been entrusted with seeing that it reached its destination (although I could not carry out this mission, for reasons explained later in this book). Beside the political circumstances that this letter helps to illuminate, it is essential for an understanding of Ché's psychology. This has been the main reason for its incorporation into the book.

The reader will find a general account of the Latin American situation in which the protagonist takes his place and carries out his revolutionary role for almost fifteen years. I have taken advantage of Ché's celebrity in the United States to show the causes of the interminable tragedy of the peoples south of the Río Grande. My intention is to let Americans see, in Ché's extraordinary life and death, that he was not a phenomenon of Nature, coincidentally appearing in Latin America, but one of a long chain of Latin American heroes who lost their lives in the struggle for the national sovereignty, independence, and dignity of our peoples.

I wrote the first draft of this book in forty-five days, and later revised it, with the advice and assistance of two persons, to whom I wish to show my appreciation here: the Argentine newspaperman Rogelio García Lupo, who read it in Buenos Aires; and Dr. Salvador Allende, President of the Chilean Senate, who read it in Santiago, Chile.

I have never looked for renown as a writer. I consider myself only a militant politician who has had the luck to live at a crucial moment—that of Latin America's liberation.

Since this is my exclusive preoccupation, it will serve as an excuse for any formal defects in the makeup of this book.

In the future, my friend will have better writers give their attention to his life, which deserves it. But it was necessary to pass on his personal and political message here and now.

R. R.

BUENOS AIRES, MAY 1968

Contents

part one

DISCOVERING LATIN AMERICA

1

Revolution in the Clouds

A number of Argentines, their names unknown to me, were living in La Paz, Bolivia, when I arrived as a political refugee in 1953. Some were army pilots who had landed there two years before, exiled after an unsuccessful insurrection against President Juan Peron, and now they were building an asphalt road between Santa Cruz and Cochabamba. Others were adventurers who spent their time under an open sky, panning for gold between the crags of the Tipuani River. Also living there was an important member of the political opposition in the Argentine parliament, Isaías Nougués, the leader of a provincial party which he generously subsidized with profits from a sugar plantation owned by his family.

It was at the home of Nougués, the richest and most influential of all the Argentines in La Paz, that I met one evening a fellow Argentine named Ernesto Guevara.

Guevara was twenty-five years old, a physician with one absorbing side-interest: archeology.

Nougués's house was in Calacoto, a residential suburb where prominent personalities of the new politics were settling. We

15

used to eat *locro*, a stew made with corn on the cob and chunks of meat which at once satisfied the host's ample appetite and served to entertain and feed friends from his own country.

The first time I saw him, Guevara didn't particularly impress me. He spoke little, preferring to listen to the conversation of others. But then, suddenly, he would cut the speaker down with a disarming smile and a razor-sharp comment.

The night we met, we walked back to La Paz together and became friends, although the only thing we really had in common at the time was that we were both young university students pressed for money. I wasn't interested in archeology, nor he in politics, at least not in the sense that politics had meaning for me then and would later have for him.

The night provided an impressive view as we left Calacoto. The neighboring hills, eroded by time, have assumed the curious shapes of organ pipes. Their strange silhouettes, outlined against the sky like a gigantic cathedral, gave the night a tragic solemnity.

We walked the six miles uphill to La Paz, discussing our plans, recalling past experiences. Guevara told me about a trip he had made a short time back, when he tried to get to Christmas Island, twenty-two hundred miles out in the Pacific Ocean, with the intention of working in the leprosarium of Rapa-Nui.

It had been a "serious trip," as he put it. He distinguished it in this way from a previous one, when he had covered twelve provinces in Argentina on a small motorcycle, a trip that had made sports news in the pages of *El Gráfico*, a popular mechanics magazine.

The "serious" trip had also started on a motorcycle. Guevara, then studying in his last year of medicine, ended up in Temuco, Chile, along with a physician named Alberto Granados. He intended to proceed on to Valparaíso with his friend and undertake the crossing from there to Christmas Island. But there were no regularly scheduled trips to the island, and no doctors were needed at the leprosarium, Guevara wasn't sure why. So they continued traveling, sleeping one night in the Chuquicamata Mine; once in Peru, they visited Machu-Picchu, a real treat for Guevara the archeologist. Guevara told me he had suffered a strong attack of asthma then. It was the first time I'd heard he was a victim of that painful ailment. The "serious" trip had continued with a rough ride on the Amazon, as far as Iquitos, from where they set out for the leprosarium of San Pablo. This place made a remarkable impression on Guevara.

"Why?" I asked him.

"Because the highest forms of human solidarity and loyalty arise among lonely and desperate men," he answered.

The lepers rewarded the young doctors' fraternal visit with their own labor in a demonstration of hopeless affection. They built them a raft to cross the Amazon, and christened it "Mambo-Tango," naming it after two types of popular music to illustrate the tie between temperate and tropical America.

The adventure was continued by raft to an insignificant port in Colombia called Leticia, where Guevara and his friend Granados found work as trainers of a local soccer team. They were soon able to go on to Bogotá by air and from there to Caracas, where they split up. After three weeks in Venezuela Guevara shipped to Miami aboard a boat used to transport horses. He stayed there briefly and finally returned to Buenos Aires to continue his medical studies. He wrote a doctoral thesis on allergies, passed examinations in twelve different subjects, and was graduated as a physician, all in a period of six months.

So he was a doctor when I met him, but no one would have guessed it, seeing him as I did that first night. I accompanied him to his place, a squalid room in a large, run-down pension in Yanacocha street. Guevara could live in the most sinister places and still maintain a sense of humor that ran off into sarcasm and irony.

Guevara took pleasure in warm, intimate conversation with friends. Although he pulled back and became satirical when with a large group of people whom he didn't know very well, he could still be a fluent and seductive conversationalist in small groups.

During those long nights in La Paz I told him my own story, which contained fewer ups and downs than his, although it too had been intense.

In the winter of 1953 I had made a remarkable escape from a police headquarters prison in Buenos Aires. I had been taken prisoner ten days before, at a time when the political police were investigating an opposition movement, trying to establish its extent and, above all, whether officers of the armed forces maintained close ties with it. Jailed and subjected to repeated interrogations, I decided that I had to escape somehow. I made up my mind one afternoon when a series of dynamite explosions interrupted a speech by President Peron to a crowd of workers gathered in front of the government house, in the Plaza de Mayo. Although there was no conclusive evidence that I had been involved in the terrorist acts, I was prisoner of a police apparatus that had to demonstrate its efficiency in some way. Therefore, after thinking over my plan several times, I escaped quietly while the guard thought I was sitting on the toilet. I went out into the street slowly, and without any outside assistance I obtained political asylum in the Guatemalan Embassy. There I could feel safe at last.

I was looking for freedom, and I had risked being caught in the streets like a cornered animal. I was a lawyer, twenty-nine years old, the son of rural landowners. Many of my political friends were in the opposition. I had been active in a commission formed by the largest opposition party—the Radical Civic Union

(*Unión Cívica Radical*)—for the purpose of defending political and union prisoners.

This commission, made up of four lawyers, was headed by Arturo Frondizi, at that time my friend and, without question, the inspirer of a generation of young politicians who would take over the government a few years later. But in 1953 Frondizi was merely a rising figure within a party marked by a single motivation: opposition to the government of General Peron.

The radical movement had behind it a long record of services to the country. It could boast that it had carried the nationalist colors in economic as well as international politics. It could prove that it had pushed social legislation and had rallied the support of hundreds of thousands of workers. But in 1953 the radical party had no way of proving that the principles of political action for which it had fought on so many occasions were being betrayed or scrapped by Peron's government.

There was an insurmountable contradiction between the need to carry out a politics of opposition and the party's half-knowledge that it could not really attack the government for failing to do something that it was, in fact, doing. For my generation this contradiction became clear much too late, and it was never clear to some. We were young, we were innocent, and we ended up condemning Peron's government for a series of characteristics that were of little consequence. We didn't realize this at the time, and, although we were convinced about our place on the Left, we rejected the thought that the Peronista working class and the ideal Left we had in mind might have anything in common.

The impulse that made us leave Argentina can probably be traced to this myopia which afflicted an entire generation. We had motives other than personal ones: we were sure there existed a common goal for all Latin America, but we felt this goal could not be reached from Argentina, a country isolated at this particular time because of its government, and isolated in general because of its exclusive ties with Europe.

We wanted to uncover authentic values, and we wanted to allow a considerable margin for adventure. These two components were mixed in unequal proportions, depending on the occasion and the individuals involved, but the connection between them continued unbroken for that generation of university students to which Ernesto Guevara and I belonged.

Authentic values and adventure. Guevara and I spoke of both on more than one occasion.

Four weeks had gone by since the day I escaped and found political asylum in the embassy of the leftist regime of Guatemala, when the Argentine government decided I could leave the country. Ismael González Aŕevalo, the Guatemalan ambassador, was a nationalist with a clear sense of purpose: he denounced the aggression that was being prepared against his country, naming those who were responsible, and did not hesitate to use the columns of the Peronista newspapers for this end. He embodied Latin American revolution both in theory and practice, and one morning he was able to take me in his car to Ezeiza Airport and put me on the airplane that would set me down safely in Chile, on the other side of the Andes.

The President of Chile at this time was a friend of Peron's, General Carlos Ibáñez, who added to his unfounded reputation as an inflexible strongman the false rumor that he was supported by one part of the Chilean Left and opposed by the other. In Ibáñez were reproduced, on a smaller scale, the good and the bad, the progress and the retrogression that distinguished Peron's government. Chile's Left wing also reflected the impact on this government of Peron's myths and manias, hopes and frustrations. It was a regime trapped by its own contradictions and, even more, by the contradictions of the society whose problems it was trying to solve.

To a young man who leaves Argentina for the first time, seeing the spurs of the Andes is a dizzying experience, and not just because of the altitude. The melancholy, rawboned, proud, and at the same time humble, faces of the Chilean people was my first concrete image of the Latin American race, that mysterious and explosive human product, so varied and yet so similar throughout the different latitudes of the continent.

It was in Chile, on my return from a visit to the tunnels of El Teniente mine, that I heard on the radio the news that the Argentine terrorists with whom I had been tried in Buenos Aires now had a following: in Santiago, Cuba, a group of university students intermingling with the Carnival crowd had attacked a military barracks. It was a brief newsflash, but one from which you could draw the conclusion—as the newscaster evidently had —that violent political upheavals in Cuba were imminent.

Having left Chile eight days after the Cuban students' attack on the Moncada barracks, I arrived in La Paz, Bolivia, where the nationalist revolution was noisily celebrating a long-awaited event: the passing of the agrarian reform law. This made the Bolivian government the second on the continent, after the Mexican, to show the courage to make such a profound decision.

Bolivia has the highest capital in the world. The altitude and the climate of Bolivia's tableland, seemingly uninhabitable and yet the location of the country's main cities, shape the character of the people. The effect of Bolivia's tragic counterpoint, man against nature, is easily observed in her political life, for the presidency of the Republic is frequently the antechamber of violent death, and men kill and die with a terrible despair, as if they wanted to finish it all as quickly as possible.

In 1953, however, popular exuberance had reached a peak in Bolivia, and its nationalist government had carried out two fundamental reforms in a little over a year: it had nationalized the country's tin mines, the largest in the world, and had made reforms in land ownership. It was hoped that these government measures would basically change the economic structure of the country, which had been fossilized by the *latifundia*, large estates where the land was worked under a feudal or semifeudal system. Agricultural production was very low in Bolivia, with three million people eking out a miserable existence, something that was inexplicable in a people who were descended directly from the Incas and who had followed with pride the motto: Don't steal, don't lie, don't be lazy.

The future of land ownership was a question implanted as deeply on the Bolivian conscience as that of the future of the people themselves. The Aymará culture, predominantly agricultural, had sought the most efficacious exploitation of the land, considering it everyone's property. The Aymarás were primitive communists, although they had clung to the idea of private property where movable goods were concerned. The Inca, or Quechua, civilization, which succeeded it, had perfected the agricultural system it had inherited, creating new institutions such as the *ayllú*,whereby all the descendants of a single ancestor collectively worked the land they had inherited together. This institution had become so deeply ingrained that in 1953 it still survived in some parts of the country. Following Quechua, the Spanish conquistadores destroyed the system of communes, which they had earlier promised to respect; thus the natives became serfs, dispossessed of their centuries-old inheritances. In the nineteenth century, Simon Bolívar, the liberator, proclaimed the country's independence, granting the Indians the lands they had occupied. Bolívar was carrying out an act of justice while also trying to avoid a renewal of upheavals like the social wars that at one point paralyzed the War of Independence in Venezuela. This experience, showing that social stability and maximum production have a solid foundation in a common exploitation and ownership of the land, was disregarded by Bolivian rulers during the second half of the nineteenth century. The despot Melgarejo declared that the lands of the Indian communities belonged to the State; thus he confiscated them, only to sell them immediately at ridiculously low prices among his court favorites. Agricultural labor then fell into a state of chaos that grew steadily worse until the nationalist government dictated a reform law in 1953. This law specified that all citizens over eighteen years of age who dedicated or wished to dedicate themselves to agriculture would be granted lands at once. This was certainly a revolutionary law, but since there were practically no foreign holders of rural land in Bolivia, it was evident that once the government had overcome internal resistance, it could promulgate this law without risk of international reprisals.

This internal resistance had been very powerful. Only a year before, during Holy Week, a force made up mostly of miners and peasants, army deserters and whole police units, had fought under the banner of the MNR, the Nationalist Revolutionary Movement, and had defeated the old professional army.

The destruction of the army, the establishment of a government in which workers and peasants were strongly represented, and the sanction and enforcement of two significant laws—nationalization of mines and agrarian reform—followed each other like an inevitable sequence taken from the most orthodox revolutionary texts. This extraordinary phenomenon, which we were to witness as we would a stage drama, contained yet another cause for admiration. After long centuries of submission an Indian people was raising its head and fighting with force of arms to recover the dignity and inheritance it had lost. This was the drama. The participants moved ceaselessly through the sloping streets of La Paz, the city walled in by mountains. Up and down the narrow, twisting lanes, between colonial houses, in an atmosphere in which it was difficult to separate the smell of frying food from the smell of gunpowder, went the *cholas* (native women of mixed Indian and European blood), each carrying her child on her back. As they walked along, they spun their llama or vicuña wools, dyed in vivid colors—the same women who recently had loaded their men's guns, fought in the streets, and even fired rifles.

I used to watch from a window in the Hotel Austria, behind the Quemado Palace, the seat of government. It was, of course, the best spot available, because during those days all the demonstrations were bound to end up at the government house.

The people formed into columns that bore some resemblance to military formations. There was a noisy gaiety that contrasted with the respect due their automatic weapons—an expansive gaiety that created bonds between strangers, that overflowed into the streets and continued after the actual occasion for their congregating had passed. The delegations went in and out of the Palace, their leaders disappeared in the distance, while the people danced in the streets. From time to time, the guards checked to make sure that the gatherings were friendly, and at daybreak you could often hear machine-gun fire; it was impossible to guess what it meant.

At the time I met him, Guevara shared his miserable little room in La Paz with "Calica" Ferrer, a student from Córdoba, Argentina, who met his basic requirements for a good traveling com-companion. For Guevara, a traveling companion should be prepared to walk for long stretches at a time, to dismiss any preoccupation about dress, and to bear without complaint the total absence of money. If these points were satisfied, everything else was of minor importance. At this time "Calica" Ferrer complied with these rules, although they apparently wore him out in the end, as we'll see farther on.

In the bare-walled room on Yanacocha Street, a few nails held up Guevara's clothes and a small bag, worn and darkened by constant use.

Guevara did not really spend much time in that corner of a crowded neighborhood of La Paz. He spent his days in the noisy cafés along 16 de Julio Avenue, and in the Camacho market, where we bought large, tropical fruit for lunch.

There was also the bar of the Sucre Palace Hotel, the most luxurious in the city, which Guevara would enter with monumental unconcern about his slovenly appearance. Seated at the tables scattered about the terrace we could watch the endless parade of the Bolivian people at a time of revolution: the *cholas,* with their children on their backs; old Indians selling furs, consumed by the sun and by *coca;* groups of peasants stumbling along because they weren't accustomed to walking on smooth pavement; and men in their Sunday clothes, most of them representatives from the mines, having just settled some matter for their fellow workers in one of the government departments.

The parade would halt at corners, where huge posters explained the new economic measures. These posters were written in defiant fighting prose, for there was no doubt that the nationalist regime contained in its ranks the most formidable array of agitators in the history of Bolivia. The "exploiter" and the "moneylender" merited the harshest words and the worst threats: these were the enemies of the common man, who, identifying his enemies from the posters, received new political education from the city walls every day.

One of these Nationalist Revolutionary Movement posters threatened any party member who attended night clubs or other nocturnal amusement spots with the punishment of relief from duties and expulsion from the party. The euphoria of power, power recently won by force of arms, ran through the Bolivian revolutionaries.

Such popular indoctrination couldn't disguise the Movement's enormous naïveté. It recommended good habits to those who had no other choice but going to bed early, and it didn't bother the new class taking form under the wing of the revolution's flag.

We had dinner very late one night at Nougués's house. It was a "reserve" meal, to quote Guevara, who could go without eating for three whole days as easily as he could stay at a table piled with all sorts of food for ten hours at a time. Now that I think back, this way of nourishing himself was one of Guevara's most impressive characteristics. Like a savage he would eat amounts of food it was hard to measure, taking all the time in the world and indulging in a sensuality he couldn't suppress. Then he would go through an ascetic period, never by choice, of course, but because of lack of funds and the occasional absence of invitations.

We had had dinner and drinks, and someone offered to take us back to La Paz. Passing through a small town called Obrajes, we all failed to notice a patrol ahead. A round of gun-shot scuffed our tires and jerked us back to reality. There, in the cold of a quiet, clear night, stood three threadbare Indians with smoking guns, asking who we were.

"Men of peace," Guevara answered, rolling down the window on his side of the car.

"Where are you coming from?" they asked with suspicion.

"From filling our bellies," Guevara went on, and after a pause, lowering his voice, ". . . they were very empty."

They allowed us to leave, after assuming serious expressions to inspect some documents whose writing they undoubtedly could not decipher. We were thoughtfully going over the dramatic situation of Bolivia in arms when, at a turn in the road, a neon sign and music filtering out into the street brought us up to the favorite cabaret of the Government's bureaucrats, The Golden Rooster. Our car slowed down as we drove past it, since we didn't want to risk a repetition of what had just happened, but no one shot at our tires from The Golden Rooster, no one there was thinking that the outcome of the revolution might be at stake. This could occur only to Indians in Obrajes, stiff with cold. Guevara winked and said, in a grim voice: "The MNR is having a good time . . ."

The MNR was indeed having a good time. But the scarcity of revolutionary cadres, the growing weight of duties falling on the shoulders of a small group of leaders, the new crop of opportunists and favorites, were so obvious that only the people's tremendous euphoria made them overlook the potential dangers to the revolution.

At one point, we decided to get a direct, personal impression of the revolutionary staff. Guevara believed our best bet would be to interview the Minister of Peasant Affairs, a lawyer named Ñuflo Chávez. He was near our own age, had a broad, intelligent face, and had been persecuted for his defense of union and political prisoners during the previous regime.

In spite of the good omens the interview was conventional and cold. The Ministry had its offices in a typical government building, poorly lit, and dirty because thousands of persons were constantly trooping through. There were long lines of silent Quechua and Aymará Indians, features blasted by the sun and the wind, long, impenetrable faces. They wore sandals, trousers made of coarse material, and jackets of exotic native fabrics. Many of them covered their heads with multicolored caps of woven wool. This was the long line of agrarian reform, Indians waiting to be given the property the newly enacted law had promised them. The column entered the building and snaked down a dark corridor. At its end a *cholo* standing on a box put a large rubber spray hose down the back of each Indian. It was a methodical task and it left each one covered with a fine powder. The Indians went on waiting, but now they seemed to be sprinkled with flour, whitened, but with the same stony expression as before; to us this operation seemed tremendously humiliating. Guevara became gloomy and shot out one of those biting comments that usually came to him when the human condition affected him deeply: "The MNR is carrying out the DDT revolution."

With this prologue our interview with the minister in charge of the peasants could not be more than polite, which probably bothered the revolutionary minister as much as it did his visitors. Guevara finally asked why this operation was conducted in such a humiliating way. The minister admitted that it was deplorable, but that the Indians were ignorant of the use of soap and couldn't be initiated to the advantages of it overnight; therefore, the only course left to the revolutionaries was to attack the effects of this ignorance with the method we had just witnessed.

We left the ministry unable to erase from our minds the sight of hundreds of vermin-infested Indians being doused by a bureaucrat with the same method used on farm animals in the suburbs of Buenos Aires. Standing in the street before a statue of Bolívar, Guevara summed up his feelings:

"The question is one of fighting the causes and not just being satisfied with getting rid of the effects. This revolution is bound to fail if it doesn't manage to break down the spiritual isolation of the Indians, if it doesn't succeed in reaching deep inside them, stirring them right down to the bone, and giving them back their stature as human beings. Otherwise, what's the use?"

In those days, Guevara was by no means a Marxist. He didn't even seem to give politics a second thought. He felt a great deal of contempt for petty politics in Argentina and took enormous pleasure in backing our friend Nougués into a corner whenever he harped, with his exile's persistence, on the causes of his disagreement with Peron. Nougués would exaggerate his misfortunes and build up his personal sacrifices in the cause of freedom, until Guevara would put down the huge spoon he used for our friend's delicious *locro* and ask him:

"Well, well. That's just fine. And now why don't you tell us a little about your sugar refineries?"

Before he had read any theoretical writings, his own observation and analysis gave him a new perspective: he saw at first-hand the importance of economic events in the history of nations and individuals. His travels through Latin America showed him the social panorama created by economic events.

If I had to describe Guevara as he was then, I'd say he was only yet feeling his way toward what he wanted to do with his life; but he was absolutely sure of what he did *not* want it to be. His own family provided a good basis for the development of his personality, even in its contradictions. The families of his father, Guevara Lynch, and his mother, de la Serna, sprang from old aristocratic lines dating back to the days before Argentina's independence. But both sides of the family had lost the major part of their landholdings, and Ché's parents had to start out on their own to build up a position as a middle class family, beginning at a very modest level.

In this case an aristocratic background proved a handicap, for what his father sensed as commitments to his past prevented him, on more than one occasion, from taking advantage of good business opportunities. The thorough conviction that an *hidalgo* or nobleman cannot lower himself to do unethical things, whatever the practices of the business world, pinned Ché's father between two alternatives: making money or continuing to be a gentleman, as his ancestors had been. He chose the second course, and it was this generous spirit that Ché inherited, raising it to such a high level that it could find expression only in social revolution and the spread of justice throughout the world. The Guevara family was socially broad-minded and democratic, intellectually active and progressive in politics, without ever losing sight of its roots in the old aristocracy. Because of his family background Ché could have been accepted as a peer by the great families of the landed aristocracy in Córdoba or Buenos Aires. Because of his economic situation his playmates were the sons of government officials and school teachers, or caddies on the greens near his house.

A family with these characteristics was bound to be troubled by the war in Spain, which broke out when Ché was eight years old. The Spanish Civil War shook Argentina as if it were its own conflict, splitting the country into "fascists" and "loyalists." The streets of Buenos Aires and the large cities in the provinces became scenes of armed scuffles and popular demonstrations that, on more than one occasion, could not be handled by a military government of the extreme Right. An uncle of Ché's, a cultured poet, felt the convulsion of that distant war and traveled to Spain. On his return he wrote a book, *Spain in the Hands of the People*, that eventually influenced Ché's conversion to Communism. Ché's mother and father were both irreligious, with the over-aggressiveness that marks those who have been educated in religious schools—his mother's education had taken place under the supervision of very strict Catholic nuns.

In this family atmosphere certain things were taken for granted: a passion for justice, the rejection of fascism, religious indifference, an interest in literature and love of poetry, and a prejudice against money and the ways of making it. The family also had a personal rebelliousness which, when combined with a gradual understanding of social problems, would lead Ché to his most important role, that of the revolutionary. One thing was certain: he didn't want anyone to kill whatever good there was in him.

But in 1953 Guevara's main curiosities were scientific, beginning with archeology. Thus, he announced to me one day that he was going to see the Gate of the Sun, a relic of Aymará culture that preserves intact the image of a brilliant civilization. Guevara didn't count on me for such interests; I doubt that he counted on any of the friends he had then. But in the cafe gatherings, he had met a remarkable German photographer, Gustav Thörlichen, and they made the trip together. The German was traveling in a military jeep equipped with outsized tires that helped him clear the mud of the bad roads. He was preparing a book of photographs of the thousand-year-old ruins of Tiahuanacu, and Guevara, who already knew Machu-Picchu and had accumulated an exceptional knowledge about the subject, was a made-to-order companion and guide.

Perhaps so as not to seem too self-indulgent, he proposed on his return that he and I visit the great mines, Siglo XX and Catavi, in the Oruro region. The big battle of the revolution between the workers and the army had taken place at these mines. On a field named simply María Barzola, the miners' dynamite had opposed the soldiers' machine guns. We had friends who worked for the Minister of Mines, Juan Lechín, and they obtained permits for us to enter the mining district.

Around this same time Lechín had said, "The revolution is more deep-rooted in Bolivia than in Guatemala or China." These miners, their numbers decimated by silicosis before they reached thirty, were the true heirs of Lechín's "revolution." Would they be able to fulfill it?

Guevara had his doubts. The day they explained to him that the government had indemnified the miners when it nationalized the mines, he made some gloomy observations. Such a step had made nationalization a mere change of bosses. As far as he was concerned, it was a grave error to confuse the requisites of a nation in arms with those of a commercial enterprise that changes hands. The Bolivians explained that the step had been prompted by a slight motive of demagogic reward and a much greater one of encouraging higher spending, for the miners had immediately invested their indemnizations in food and clothing. But Guevara insisted that the act of recovering the mines had been clouded by this arrangement because it had gratified the senses at a historical moment when it was more imperative to raise morale. He was inflexible on this point, concluding that, for a small reward, the miners had reduced the material and moral reserves of a revolution that would in time need everything it had won.

Not one of our Bolivian friends could change this judgement.

We decided to leave Bolivia for Peru, by truck. Ours would be one of those tough trucks without shock absorbers, trucks that unload their products in the Indian street markets and transport the Indians back and forth, piled in with sacks of salt and sugar, bags of potatoes and *coca* leaves, and an occasional stick of dynamite.

Our plan was to cross into Peru overland, skirting Lake Titicaca as far as Copacabana, the tourist town and sailing resort eighty-five miles from La Paz.

The three of us—"Calica" Ferrer was still a member of the group—went to buy the tickets, and Guevara struck up an enlightening conversation with the ticket clerk. The man sat behind a grimy desk. His skin was shiny, and he wore a handkerchief carefully rolled around his neck, to keep his collar clean. He must have been surprised to see three white men before him.

"You'll be traveling via Panagra, right?"

"What do you mean 'via Panagra'?" Guevara asked. "We're going by truck, to Copacabana."

"Yes, by truck, but in Panagra Class, right?"

We looked at one another without understanding. On a peeled wall, an ancient Panagra calendar showed Miami Beach.

Then the *cholo* explained that Panagra Class was the driver's compartment, a cabin where four or five privileged passengers were crushed in together and had to pay extra for the privilege. This was the only possible place, the *cholo* insinuated, for three young white men, who could not be expected to mix with the

Indians. Guevara understood immediately and cut the discussion short.

"No, no Panagra for us. We're traveling in the back, like everybody else."

The trip was an indispensable step in our education about Indian America. We entered a hostile world and were trapped between bundles and people who looked like bundles. Silence. Bruising jolts and silence. We discovered that it was impossible to try and show the sympathy we felt before those scrutinizing, metallic eyes, those lips clamped together forbiddingly, refusing to answer our questions. From time to time, a mouth would gape and let out a foul breath of chewed *coca*, a breath it didn't seem possible could have fermented inside a human body.

We couldn't establish a semblance of human communication with the Indians, yet the guards at the Peruvian border were absolutely convinced that we had turned their heads with ideas about agrarian revolution. On September 11, 1953, when we stepped onto Peruvian soil, the border police at Yunguyo, the first town after leaving Bolivia, discovered that our luggage consisted almost exclusively of books and pamphlets put out by the Bolivian revolutionaries. The propaganda material had been handed to us by Chávez, the minister, during our interview. One of the Peruvian police asked, "Are you agitators?"

Guevara answered, "Hardly. We don't speak a word of Aymará or Quechua, and we couldn't wring a word out of these guys during the whole trip."

Still, we lost a lot of time before we could convince the guards that our intentions were harmless and that we didn't plan to contaminate the Indians of Peru with the germs of the agrarian revolution. Actually, these crude border guards had learned to see the problem correctly, and inadvertently they gave us a free lesson in history: political frontiers never succeed in dividing human masses faced with the same problems; an agrarian revolution that flares up among the Indian masses of one country does not burn out at the political limits fixed by white men in far-away cities. The winds of Indian rebellions were blowing on the Peruvian border in 1953, and the customs men suspected that we were bringing more fuel in our shabby packs.

We were given safe-conducts and continued on to Juliaca, and from there to Cuzco. Guevara wanted to confirm a hypothesis he had formed on a previous stay in Machu-Picchu. Somewhat contemptuous of our ignorance of archeology, he reported his theory very carefully despite our discreet scepticism. We crossed the valley of Urubamba and wandered over the ruins of Sacsahuamán, a walled fortress before which Guevara succumbed: he immediately decided to stay there, while I went on to Lima, the capital.

Peru at that time was ruled by a decided reactionary, General Manual Ordía. He had risen to power unscrupulously and stayed in power the same way. A massacre in the city of Arequipa had spattered him with the blood of hundreds and had left him only more implacable. Víctor Raúl Haya de la Torre, the head of APRA, had been in asylum in the Colombian Embassy for four years, and the number of policemen reported in the streets of Lima was exceptionally high. The opposition could not protest: demonstrations by the political parties had been broken up with police clubs, and the student movement was having great difficulties, with many of its leaders in prison. Some had been exiled and others subjected to tortures.

The way things looked, my situation wasn't very promising. My passport was really no more than the safe-conduct of an asylee at the Guatemalan Embassy, and in Peru anyone coming from countries with agrarian revolutions was suspect. Because of the incident at the border my authorization to enter Peru carried the requirement that I present myself to the police in Lima as soon as I arrived there. And it's common knowledge that the police make a profession of being suspicious.

In the company of some American newsmen from the *Chicago Tribune*, who visited only the big hotels and some of the ruins, I crossed the Andes, that mass of bare rock covered with snow, on whose sides the war for independence was fought. The number of miserable towns grew as we got closer to the capital; the small streets in the suburbs were filled with people, and the colorful clothing of the Indians was suddenly as dazzling as the sunlight.

Lima can often give a wrong impression of the country. The power of Spain and the civilization it transplanted to America have been symbolized for three centuries by the splendid architecture of the Cathedral, the Torre-Tagle Palace, and the University of San Marcos, the oldest in America and fertile ground for student movements. But Lima's wealth has nothing to do with the rest of the country, which in 1953 was populated by nine million inhabitants. Half of these were direct descendants of the primitive Indian settlers, and a very high percentage of the rest was made up of *mestizos* with Indian and European blood.

Naturally, there was no pity for this multitude of Indians and *mestizos*. Economic events had silently crushed millions of human beings and condemned them to slave labor in the fields and in the mines.

A million peasants, chained to the land of two thousand *latifundia,* supported the wealth and badly managed administration of a ridiculous aristocratic minority, ally to bankers, importers, and foreign investors.

This police dictatorship, maintained in power by a wealthy few in order to preserve their economic status, was a crushing reality. I decided to go on with my trip without waiting for Guevara. He had given me an address where I could find him in Lima, the house of a nurse he had known in a hospital in Buenos Aires, but he hadn't shown up there yet.

Luck brought us together again. In the ticket line for the bus to Tumbes, a town on the border of Ecuador, a fellow was smoking a cigarette and distractedly watching those who passed near him. It was Guevara. We gave each other a bear hug, and after buying our tickets for the next day's bus, went out to say goodbye to the city of Lima. There was a party at the Colombian Embassy: Haya de la Torre, still in asylum, was receiving his friends. In the street outside, tanks and troop trucks exaggerated the diplomatic interdict provoked by the presence of the popular refugee. Guevara shook his head and said: "Why are they so scared of him? After all, he's just like anybody else . . ."

We left the next day, our bus following the coast road, passing through Trujillo, Piura and Talara, in an arid desert swept by north winds, where the flow of oil never stops.

A climate of war prevailed in Tumbes, a lagoon that marks the border between Peru and Ecuador. The armies of the two countries were showing each other their latest weaponry. This military charade was prolonged by a border dispute that seemed at times to be kept alive solely to justify the acquisition of further armament and the expansion of military forces.

"Better be careful with these guys," Guevara warned, looking at the guns uneasily. "They're such poor shots that if a bullet gets away from them, who knows where it will end up."

On September 16, 1953, the border police of Ecuador registered the entry of Ernesto Guevara, "Calica" Ferrer, and myself into the country at Huaquillas, an Indian village. From there we proceeded to Puerto Bolívar and then on to Guayaquil.

No one can say he really knows the tropics unless he has been in Guayaquil. Situated on the Guayas River, about forty miles upstream from its mouth, the city is less than a foot above sea level. Mangrove thickets enclose it, the waters stagnate, and the classic diseases thrive: malaria, intestinal parasitism, and yellow fever. At the time we arrived, the city had fewer than four hundred thousand inhabitants, miserably lodged in wooden houses half-rotted away and invested with termites. We discovered with horror that this clutter of poorly lit houses could be reduced to ashes in a matter of minutes; fire engines dashed through the streets, offering the daily spectacle of their dramatic race against incineration.

We were in the so-called "dry season," no doubt a figure of speech to distinguish those months when it rained at least an hour in the middle of each day from the other months of the year when a heavy curtain of water submerged the streets and the avenues under tons of mud.

Our group was joined by three Argentine students, all of them studying law, Oscar Valdovinos, Gualo García, and Andre Herrero. They had arrived in Guayaquil a few days before and had read the news, practically buried in the middle of the newspaper, of the arrival in the city of an Argentine exile and two friends. We met at the University, exchanged addresses, and discovered at the same time that the general state of our personal finances was disastrous. Consequently, we decided immediately that we would all share one room in a wooden house next to the port.

It was a room with two rickety beds. Their use was a strict arrangement, first come first served; in the morning there were always four bodies stretched out on the floor, barely covered by one sheet. Our sleep was sometimes broken by the feet of a passing rat or small, but disgusting, vermin. We fell asleep from exhaustion, following our last stand against the mosquitoes that reproduced by the millions on the unhealthy waters of the Guayas.

Early in the morning, when the light wasn't yet very strong, we used to go and watch cargo being maneuvered into the big banana boats, the movements of the barges and tugs with products of the tropics, and the rafts floating down from the north. Around noon, a clamor of voices would sometimes begin to swell. In the beginning we were surprised, but we soon grew accustomed to seeing disorderly crowds converging on the riverbank, chanting political refrains and cheering the name of an ex-mayor of the city, Carlos Guevara Moreno, probably one of the most efficient demagogues I have ever known.

These crowds roared into the streets, rushed hard and pressed together, defying the police; but they always ended up discouraged, and finally evaporated as fast as the rain under the noon sun. They became another object of study for us, among whom, with the incorporation of the new group, politicians outnumbered scientists. They were masses ready for anything, with nothing to lose, and much too often some lost their lives in clashes with the police. But they were masses who lacked revolutionary leadership; their energy served only the creole demagogues, who quickly turned their backs on them once power was in their hands.

While we observed and discussed them, time slipped past, and we ran out of the little money we had. An emergency meeting was called, and we decided to leave that tropical sweatbox as soon as possible. To continue our journey we'd have to sell at once the few pieces of extra clothing we still owned, whatever shape they were in. With the common fund we could scrape together this way, Guevara and "Calica" Ferrer could travel to Venezuela, their original goal, while the three new friends and I would go on to Guatemala where, we agreed, a revolutionary movement of immense interest and definite historical influence was in progress.

In poor countries used clothing is sold in the streets. But there was small chance of selling ours in the streets of Guayaquil, for the best items we had left were winter wear. Valdovinos was therefore dispatched to Quito, the capital, nine thousand feet above sea level, to convert into dollars my only luxury, a vicuña topcoat I had bought in La Paz, and the threadbare, faded suits we had brought along.

Guevara kept the least: a pair of trousers deformed by constant use, a shirt that had been white at one time, and a sport jacket whose pockets had burst from carrying a variety of objects ranging from the inhaler for his asthma to the huge *plantains* that were often his only nourishment.

We were almost naked, but we could continue northward, leaving behind us the fetid waters of the Guayas, the house rats, and the stench of rotten wood and fruit. It was during these days that we tried to get the consul of Colombia to issue us tourist visas to Bogotá. But the situation in Colombia was critical. A few months before, General Rojas Pinilla had ousted the ultraconservative regime of Laureano Gómez, and in the valley of Tolima the peasant guerrillas were negotiating their surrender to the army in exchange for recognition of their right to occupy their lands. The consul wasn't about to let six foreigners, who intended crossing valleys and mountains in the middle of the war, run into trouble. He set down one condition: we must buy airline tickets to Bogotá, bearing the date we would leave the country. It was a condition our empty pockets couldn't meet. We had to give up the idea of passing through Colombia, and I had to play my last card.

It was actually a letter addressed by the Chilean socialist leader Salvador Allende to a socialist lawyer in Guayaquil; it asked him to help me in any way he could. The Chilean socialists hated Peron, and I belonged to the Left wing of a party that opposed Peron. This ideological kinship, and the friendship I had with Allende, and still have today, explain why the senator gave the letter to the young exile.

I hadn't had to use it until then, but obviously there was no other way out. I went to see the socialist lawyer with Guevara, since, in view of the request I was about to make, I thought it would be better if he saw with his own eyes the extent of our poverty. He gave us a friendly welcome, but seemed at a loss when he realized that there weren't just two travelers stranded in Guayaquil, but four more. He made two telephone calls and finally told us that we'd be given six tickets for Panama via the Great White Fleet, the United Fruit Company's steamship line.

There was one condition: it would be impossible to put six free passengers on the same ship. We would have to depart in three relays, two of us on each trip.

That night, "Calica" Ferrer, who expected to make money in the construction business, left the group. And during a friendly argument in which he put up very little resistance, no doubt carried away by our enthusiasm, Guevara gave up the idea of settling in Venezuela, where he had intended joining Doctor Granados at the San Pablo leprosarium.

"How come you're going to Venezuela," I had asked him, "when there's nothing to do there except earn dollars?"

Guevara insisted that he had made a pact with his friend Granados and he had to keep his word.

"Things are happening to Guatemala, *viejo*," I went on. "An important revolution is going on there; it's something you've got to see."

"All right," Guevara gave in, "but only on condition that we walk together." And with a slightly threatening tone, tinged by his sense of humor, he added, "Let's not get carried away by Guatemalan officialdom, shall we? I say this because you reformers are specialists in bureaucracy."

The thought that we would all meet again in Panama, to go together from there to Guatemala, put us in high spirits that night. And Guevara topped off everything by winning a bet from us. He assured us that the shorts he was wearing, the only pair he had owned in the last two months, were so impregnated with dirt from the road that they would stand by themselves without support. We didn't believe him. Guevara took off his trousers. Before our eyes was a piece of underwear that looked like a brick-layer's work pants, the fabric was so stiff and its color so incredible. He removed this also, and we had to give up. Guevara had won the bet. His shorts stood upright, and their owner promised that he would soon teach them to mark time.

On October 9, 1953, the first two of the group, Valdovinos and I, were ready to leave. At the last minute, Andro Herrero announced that he was going back to Argentina, worn out by the adventure and lonely for his family and friends. A few days later Guevara and Gualo Garcia would follow us. We were close friends; we understood one another well; camaraderie on the road and uncomfortable lodgings had set up a permanent bond between all of us.

It would seem incredible later on, but Ernesto Guevara entered the boiling-pot of Central America thanks to a trip courteously given to him by the United Fruit Company.

2

The Caribbean Storm

Since June 17, 1952—when agrarian reform was proclaimed—
Guatemala had been the major testing ground for Latin American
revolution, a more significant model than the Bolivian revolution.
Its importance sprang from a basic distinction between the two
movements: in Bolivia, the land to be distributed belonged to
the big creole landowners, and in Guatemala it belonged to U. S.
corporations with powerful political influence.

Between 1821, when its independence was declared, and 1944,
when the process of national revolution began, Guatemala had
had only two constitutionally elected governments. Continual
seizure of power and joint control by the landowning class and
foreign capital marked its history. Servitude, obscurantism, and
miserable living conditions were the disheartening issues of this
system. At the time of the agrarian revolution, eight out of every
ten inhabitants went without shoes, and seven out of every ten
were illiterate. The country's feudal lords, in league with
American capitalists, hypocritically lamented the consequences
of this situation and falsely blamed it on the fact that half of
Guatemala's population was Indian—despite the fact that most

Guatemalan Indians descended from the Mayas, whose civilization was anything but unimpressive. Thus, the system that despoiled an entire nation convinced it with propaganda that its own inhabitants were the cause of its ills. By undermining national morale and encouraging resignation and fatalism, the alliance between the country's magnates and foreign millionaires could drain the wealth from the land indefinitely.

In 1944 a coalition of young army officers and intellectuals with vague projects for reform took over the government. They started with no ambitious plan for the future, but with the realization that Guatemala was bogged down in a desperate existence and, as a people, had squandered its inheritance. The Mayas knew how to write, they painted beautifully, and they carved stone sculptures and worked in ceramics. The codices, temples, and archeological fragments scattered throughout the country attested to the quality of Mayan civilization. Spanish and capitalist colonizations had destroyed the best products of that civilization. They had plunged the Indian population into poverty and ignorance, although retaining important elements of social and historical cohesion. But for the young officers and intellectuals in 1944, a new period was opening, and theirs was an attempt to save half the population of Guatemala and integrate it into a national state.

The purpose of most of the government's new measures was recognition of the Indians as citizens with the same rights as the white descendants of European settlers. One after the other the pillars of the old order were pulled down—especially servitude and the system of private loans to the Indians. On the whole these reforms were supported by the majority of those who had any voice in the matter.

But the fact remained that any modification of the social status quo was bound to affect the economic privileges of the more than one thousand landowners who held over half of the country's best lands. The biggest of these was the United Fruit Company, the famous American banana monopoly. In 1953 the Guatemalan government expropriated almost four hundred thousand acres of the United Fruit's land; the company, seeing the handwriting on the wall, started in motion its gigantic and well entrenched machinery of pressure and threats, and thereupon the U. S. State Department intervened and vehemently defended the company's position.

Until now, the revolution's path had followed an almost straight line. To accomplish the goal the President had implied in his definition—*"Socialists, because we live in the twentieth century, but not materialist socialists. Man is not just a stomach. We believe that, above all, he hungers for his dignity"*— the revolutionaries needed to study the economic reforms with care. They might believe in good faith that man's stomach was *not* the main thing, but they could see for themselves, day after day, that for the big economic interests the stomach *was* the main thing.

In the slow evolution that took place between 1944 and 1953, during which time many had dropped out along the way, the revolutionaries had learned a number of things in actual practice that were not explained in their books. And yet there were many other things they didn't understand until it was too late: for one, that professional soldiers grow discouraged with a revolution in a much shorter time than it takes the Indian masses to develop enthusiasm for it.

But in November 1953, when Valdovinos and I reached the port of San José, the atmosphere in Guatemala was ostensibly enthusiastic. It was only after a few days that you noticed the tension running through the conversations in the cafés and the little knots of people with fear in their voices when referring to the friction between the government and the United Fruit Company.

We had decided to continue our trip after twenty days in

Panama, waiting in vain for Guevara and Gualo García. Panama was boiling from the humid heat and fierce anti-American feelings. The temperature seemed to rise with the political passions, and the political passions grew hotter as the thermometer rose. The thought that neither the climate nor the political situation could be changed made our contact with both unbearable; after three weeks we resolved to leave.

I was traveling under a unique Argentine passport—officially it was only good for a single trip to Guatemala, the country that had given me political asylum. Really a safe-conduct, it had determined my destination, and to a degree my itinerary, from the start; and of course it ultimately placed me at the disposition of the Guatemalan authorities. Accordingly, the day after I set foot in the capital, I went to the Department of Foreign Affairs to let them know I was there. Raúl Oseguada, the Chancellor, was a teacher who had studied in Argentina, as had Arévalo. But unlike him, he had moved around in bohemian student circles and had participated in Buenos Aires night life. He had earned his living in Argentina as a musician, playing the guitar in dance hall orchestras, and he retained a fond, nostalgic memory of those years.

Chancellor Osegueda was our protector. He paid our keep in a modest boarding house near Quinta Avenida, and he introduced us to the official and political world of Guatemala.

It was a very busy world, but if examined closely, it was obvious that the regime was stuck in a quagmire of personal ambitions disguised as ideological differences. This struck us as a curious and original phenomenon: since all the different parties maintained that they were revolutionary, you had what seemed to be a multi-party democracy with everyone trying to conduct a revolution at once. Coming from Argentina, which was governed by a strong president backed by a solid party that wasn't partial to lobbying, we found Guatemala a notable contrast. The phenomenon became so obvious that it was impossible to ignore it. Only time would tell whether or not the system could support a revolutionary process.

About this time we heard that two Argentine brothers, driving from the United States to Buenos Aires in a '46 Ford, had arrived in Guatemala. The older one, Walter Beveraggi Allende, was professor of Political Economy at Boston University and had been involved in an international scandal of such proportions that Peron had finally taken away his Argentine citizenship, an action without precedent in Argentina and almost unheard of in Latin America. He was now crossing borders with an affidavit given him by the U. S. State Department, perhaps in acknowledgement of his position as professor at an American university. The younger brother, Domingo Beveraggi Allende, had escaped to Uruguay without papers and was traveling on a Uruguayan identity card on which it was stated that he was a citizen of Argentina. Naturally, we had to meet these two in some part of the world.

At this point my companion, Valdovinos, who had married a young Panamanian aristocrat after a fast courtship, decided to give up the adventure and join his wife, waiting for him in Panama. I joined the traveling brothers, with my safe-conduct pass.

Ours must have been one of the most suspicious-looking sets of identity papers ever assembled in Central America. Presented together they were enough to alarm any official, and that's exactly what happened with the consul of El Salvador, an obstinate man who looked us up and down, shaking his head. Chancellor Osegueda had to convince him that our visit to his country had a "cultural purpose."

My plan was to go back and look for Guevara and Gualo García, whom I imagined to be tied up by some administrative tangle with the authorities in Panama. There were moments when

I was afraid they hadn't even been able to get on the ship that was to take them out of Ecuador.

Since the Allende brothers were heading south, I joined them, and we began a difficult trip through the "Banana Republics," as they are called by the American press. The rainy season had started, and some stretches of the highway, the only one we could take, were flooded over. All commercial traffic was behind schedule, and many truck drivers had decided to put off their trips until the rains ended. We passed through El Salvador and on December 16 arrived at El Amatillo, on the border of Honduras; we crossed without stopping. We entered Nicaragua at Madriz, where Somoza's national guard registered our entry on December 18, 1953. We went on to Managua, and from there to Rivas, a small colonial city, where everyone we questioned agreed that we shouldn't continue south. The rains were washing out sections of the road and it was practically impossible to pass.

But my friends put the Ford on the road again and the sensible advice of the local people was lost behind us.

About ten miles from Rivas an impenetrable curtain of rain made us begin to doubt whether we'd ever make it to Piedra Blanca, the entrance to Costa Rica.

We went on, our nerves understandably strained, trying to make out the road as it proceeded through the thickest jungle in Central America. Suddenly, we made out two forms thrashing through the mud. No doubt about it: two men were coming toward us, plodding with great difficulty along the side of the road. We made up our minds to ask them about the condition of the road ahead. Just then, the air cleared enough to let us see their faces.

Ernesto Guevara and Gualo García, bags slung over their shoulders, soaked to the bone, water and sweat pouring down their faces, looked at us through the rain.

"Stop!" I yelled. My shout was heard by the driver, who pulled up, and by the walkers, who also stopped.

We threw our arms around one another, and my friends in the Ford were introduced with very little ceremony, considering the circumstances. Guevara and García gave us a hair-raising description of the road. The water had swept away embankments and bridges, and the only vehicle they had met in the last six hours was ours.

We decided that the whole group should return to Rivas. Guevara and I were delighted. We couldn't stop talking about our experiences since separating in Guayaquil, and kept interrupting this recital to make plans to return to Guatemala.

I learned that from Panama, where they had been taken by the Great White Fleet, they had continued to Costa Rica, sometimes in Mack trucks and sometimes on foot. They had been in an accident. A truck in which they were riding overturned, landing heavily in the side ditch. Guevara was thrown with great force from his unstable perch on some fruit crates and hit the ground hard. More than ten days later the muscles and tendons of his left forearm were still sore from the fall, and he had trouble using the arm.

We were almost in Rivas. It was getting dark. We stopped at a busy restaurant near the main square of the old city, where several men were smoking lazily and some girls were preparing supper. It became an unforgettable evening, with lots of *mate* (an herb-tea), and reminiscences of our country, which the "Ford brothers" converted into songs, accompanying themselves on a guitar. Around seven o'clock we were served rice and fried chicken, hot from the fire. Guevara ate slowly, following his philosophy of "reserve" food. He and his companion had gone five days without a full meal, but now the air was charged with spontaneous optimism, stirred up by our unexpected reunion and the feeling that everything would turn out right in Guatemala.

Suddenly we realized what an unexpected and curious show

we must be presenting, with our strange appearance and the Argentine folk music and songs. A silent ring grew around us as groups of children interrupted their games to take a closer look at us and listen to our singing.

"Do you know what I thought when I saw you?" Guevara asked, and answered himself immediately "I thought· What lucky bastards these Yankees are. They have a car in this goddamn rain, and we have to walk."

True, the Ford had American license plates and a special insignia that said "Boston University."

It was in Rivas, a dot on the map where years later the dictator Anastasio (Tacho) Somoza was assassinated, that our friends with the Ford decided to give up their motor trip.

We saw in the new year, 1954, in San José de Costa Rica, the most Spanish and traditional of the Central American capitals. San José had become the general headquarters for an organization called the Caribbean Legion. Its role was that of a democratic Internationale, and it had drawn some of the most famous liberals of the Caribbean area and included the President of Costa Rica, José (Pepe) Figueres, among its members. It had been formed in Cuba when Carlos Prío Socarras was President and while Rómulo Betancourt and Juan Bosch were living in Havana. Later on it had proved strong enough to obtain the presidency of Costa Rica for Otilio Ulate, Figueres' candidate, and eventually for Figueres himself. In 1952, when Batista took power in Cuba, the leaders of the Legion had abandoned that country and sought refuge in San José.

Actually, the military effectiveness of the Caribbean Legion wasn't great. Nevertheless, the repeated expeditions of Cayo Confite and Luperón against Trujillo, the Dominican dictator, had inspired an embryonic military organization in the Caribbean and taught hundreds of young men how to handle modern weapons. More important, these adventures helped to arouse the romantic enthusiasm of students throughout Central America. The Legion had developed, as far as it could, a sense of brotherhood among its members, a sense that they were citizens of a nation larger than those bounded by narrow political limits. It was a concept based on Bolívar's idea of the great Latin American nation, although for the Legion it was really restricted to the Caribbean area, its own field of action. Cubans, Hondurans, and an equal number of Dominicans organized the expeditions against Trujillo; they were armed in Cuba with that government's blessing. Several of these expeditions operated out of Guatemala with the approval of the authorities. Nationalities had been overlooked in recruiting the Legion, as in the last century, when these countries had joined forces to fight Spanish domination.

The leaders of the Legion were living in a residential suburb of San José. There, in the same house, were the Venezuelans, Rómulo Betancourt and Raúl Leoni, and the Dominican, Juan Bosch. The fact that all three would become presidents of their countries in the following years indicates the intense movement of men and ideas through that house in San José.

Betancourt was not surprised one day when Ernesto Guevara and I came to his place and asked to discuss Latin American politics with him. Betancourt's dialectic facility betrayed a Marxist background, although his skill in debate also revealed a certain authoritarian streak. It was then impossible to determine the price he was willing to pay to satisfy his ambition. His store of information and his intelligent way of explaining points of view were impressive. We struck up a good relationship, encouraged by Betancourt's frequent invitations to lunch.

These meals were good news to us at the time, and what Betancourt treated us to in a small Italian restaurant nearby would have been good news to any gourmet, anywhere, in any age. The owner of the restaurant was an Italian woman, a little ripe but still attractive, who exchanged meaningful looks with Juan Bosch while she served.

Bosch, a mulatto with a profound look in his eyes and a natural, unpretentious elegance, wrote fiction and, occasionally, history. Guevara felt an immediate attraction for Bosch and an equal dislike for Betancourt. He used to talk about Latin American literature with Bosch, including the Dominican's writings; they also discussed Cuba, to which Bosch had just dedicated an enthusiastic book as yet unpublished. Guevara, who was an omnivorous reader, laid bare his deepest and most sensitive feelings during these lunches with Bosch.

But an invisible barrier stood between him and Betancourt. I believe they were divided initially by a spontaneous antagonism and then by a conflict of ideas. Betancourt talked about the United States having a double image: a friendly face that promised understanding and assistance, and a hateful, imperialist face he said he would fight. Guevara replied that this dichotomy set up a false choice and, like all false choices, benefitted only the powerful. The two could never make any headway on the subject of relations between the United States and Latin America, although Guevara was willing to listen respectfully to Betancourt's explanations.

Exchanging conversation from table to table, we established our relations with some other political exiles. They were also young, and hadn't been in the country very long either. They made up a disorderly and noisy group, discussing politics and women with great enthusiasm; and, like us, they were having a serious financial problem in a country where they knew few important people.

These were the Cubans of the 26th of July, 1953, Movement. In that small café in January 1954, they told us disturbing stories of the massacre following the failed attack on the Moncada barracks and the terrorism in the cities that was beginning to stain the streets with blood. To both Guevara and myself, it seemed that these excited young men were living a fantasy. They talked of summary executions, dynamite attacks, military demonstrations in the universities, kidnappings, and machine-gun fire; and they talked in a way so natural that it made our heads spin. Then they would say goodbye and go calling from house to house, selling beach sandals they had made with their own hands; or else they went to cash the checks their families or friends had sent them from Cuba or the United States. It was from them that Guevara first heard about Fidel Castro.

There, in San José, they drew only a mocking incredulity from Guevara, and more than once he cut short some wild story with a sharp comment:

"Listen, why don't you tell us a cowboy movie now?"

We left Costa Rica for El Salvador by bus.

Our first stop was Santa Ana, the country's second largest city. I remembered that El Salvador's friendly ambassador to Guatemala had suggested a visit to a Colonel Vides, if I ever happened to be in Santa Ana. He turned out to be the most important man in the city and one of the most powerful in the country. We got in touch with him fast. When he learned who had sent us, he went out of his way to make our visit pleasant. We became his guests on an impressive coffee plantation called Dos Cruces (Two Crosses), intelligently cultivated with complex installations for processing the coffee. The Colonel had an exceptionally lovely daughter, who offered to show us the plantation.

As we strolled around, remarking on the efficient way the land was used, we noticed a few eye-opening details. The land was enclosed with a barbed-wire fence about six feet high and was patrolled by guards—uniformed, though not with the colors of the El Salvador army, and without insignia. They carried impressive .45 caliber revolvers, but at the time, they looked rather harmless.

The Colonel's daughter answered our curiosity. She told us the guards were the plantation's "internal" police, and their duty was to restore order at the first sign of rebellion from "those people," indicating some women and children waiting for their men outside a cluster of tumble-down shacks.

The girl's simple explanation left us dumbstruck. That night her father explained that the police were necessary because of the peasants' lack of obedience and affection for their work. As if to clarify this, he informed us that he hadn't earned his colonel's rank in military schools but in the suppression of a peasant movement twenty-five years before.

It was the last night we spent at Dos Cruces with the pleasant Colonel, who shot his workers, and his lovely daughter, who tried to convince us with the assurance "Papa is a good man."

When we reached Guatemala, the contrast struck us immediately. It was the middle of January, and the political temperature was climbing dangerously. By now our senses were well trained, and we smelled something in the air, ready to explode.

On January 29, President Arbenz charged that an invasion of his country was being plotted, that the forces were being readied in El Salvador, the Dominican Republic, Nicaragua, and Venezuela, and that the instigator of the conspiracy was a "government in the north." This declaration in itself implied a break between the governments of Guatemala and the United States—in Latin America anyone who mentions "a government in the north," even if the phrase comes from the southernmost country in the hemisphere, can be referring only to the government in Washington. The next day, with ominous speed, the State Department replied to the ministry in Guatemala that the charge was false and was part of a "Communist effort to disrupt the Tenth Inter-American Conference," to be convened in Caracas at the beginning of March.

Guevara and I stayed at the same boarding house where my friend, Chancellor Osequeda, had generously paid my bill the last time. One day the Argentine Ambassador, Nicasio Sánchez Toranzo, unexpectedly came to see us. Since I was a political refugee, he had been notified of my presence in the country by Guatemala's chancellery. But Sánchez Toranzo hadn't come to visit us as an enemy. On the contrary. He brought a token of friendship, some *yerba mate,* the best gift you could give two Argentines far from their homeland. Sánchez Toranzo was a Peronista diplomat and, moreover, had a brother who was known to be one of Peron's most devoted generals. Sánchez Toranzo's visits brought us our precious herb, which he received from Buenos Aires by air, and another priceless gift as well, newspapers from Argentina for Guevara and me to read not more than a week after publication. Sánchez Toranzo had followed the development of the revolution in Guatmelala with sympathetic eyes, but he could not hide his concern about America's reprisals. Our discussion of this led to an analysis of the relations between Peron and the government of Guatemala. At this point, the anti-Peronista sentiments Guevara and I held became disconcerting. Peron had supported the Guatemalan government all the way, and he would continue this policy, as would shortly be seen at the Conference in Caracas. To see such a close affinity between Peron and Guatemala frankly shook us up.

On this same subject, the ex-President, Juan José Arévalo, told us something we hadn't known. A short time ago, a close relative of his had died. Arévalo was ambassador to Chile at the time, and he immediately returned home. He found out through Osegueda that we were in Guatemala and one day invited us to lunch near Amatitlán, a beautiful spot twelve miles from the capital. Guevara and I questioned him in a friendly way about why he had decorated Peron with the Order of the Quetzal, the highest distinction Guatemala could award a foreigner. Arévalo told us that shortly after his own government had passed the Labor Law in May 1947, the American steamship lines had announced that they would stop serving Guatemalan ports. The country had no fleet of its own, and this decision meant a full-scale blockade. Arévalo had started a secret negotiation with Peron. Their intermediary was the Honduran economist Juan Nuñez Aguilar, who had been with Peron at the Military Academy of Argentina. Aguilar visited his old schoolmate and explained Guatemala's problem. Immediately, Peron called the head of the merchant fleet and ordered that, from then on, ships flying the Argentine flag must call at Guatemalan ports. Arévalo admitted that Peron had done even more. The first ships to touch Guatemalan ports had brought arms from the munition plants in Buenos Aires. This explanation of why Guatemala had conferred diplomatic honors on Peron left two anti-Peron men completely confused.

The cafés in Guatemala in those days were alive with rumors and American CIA agents, many of whom operated openly. There was no mystery about their headquarters and hang-outs or where and how some interesting bits of information could be sold to them for U.S. dollars. The name of a U.S. Colonel, Carl Studder, always came up in our conversations, and while many people said they had seen him, it seemed more likely that this officer worked out of Managua through a large network of spies.

In one café we met some of the Cubans Guevara and I had known in Costa Rica. Just as we did, they watched with anguish the pressures on the Guatemalan revolution, even as they prepared their own. They said that the solution to Cuba's problem would begin as soon as Fidel Castro, the leader of the 26th of July, left his prison on the Isle of Pines and joined them all in

Mexico. From there they would go to work on their own country.

Our situation was different. One day Guevara suggested that we offer to work for the Guatemalan revolution in whatever capacity we could help most. As a doctor, Guevara assumed there would be no problem to his assignment.

But when we visited the Public Health Department, with a letter of introduction from Osegueda, we discovered that the matter was more complicated than we had thought. Guevara had come to offer his services as a physician and indicated that he was interested in working in the Petén region. An interesting program of aid to the Indian population was under way there; also, one of the most magnificent examples of Mayan culture is located there, the temple of Tikal, two hundred and thirty feet high. Guevara still had his archeological curiosity.

The conversation proceeded smoothly, and Guevara considered the job his until the minister said in passing:

"By the way, do you have your card?"

"What card?" Guevara answered.

"What do you mean, what card? The PGT membership card."

"No," Guevara said, unable to hide his surprise, "I'm a revolutionary and I don't believe affiliations of this kind mean anything . . ."

"I'm sorry," the minister said, getting to his feet to indicate that the interview was over, "but it's part of the usual procedure."

"Look, friend, the day I decide to affiliate myself, I'll do it from conviction, not through obligation, understand?"

Perhaps the minister did understand, but Guevara never got a chance to practice medicine in Petén only because he wouldn't fill out an identification card of the Guatemalan Labor Party (PGT), another name for the Communist Party. The leader of the Communists had carried his party's sectarianism to such extremes that, some years later, he couldn't put up with it himself and became an anti-Communist. With the same sectarianism, of course.

The colony of Latin American exiles in Guatemala included a dynamic and well-established group of Peruvian members of APRA. These Peruvians had been distributed among the organizations responsible for economic and agrarian planning, two areas in which many of them were experts. Our friendly sessions with them brought Guevara together with Hilda Gadea, a girl with an exotic face showing traces of both Indian and Chinese blood in proportions difficult to figure out. Hilda Gadea was working for INFOP, an institute created by the revolution to stimulate agrarian and industrial production. Eventually, she had a daughter by Guevara and married him in Mexico. But at the beginning of 1954 she was only an unselfish companion of the exiles, and Guevara soon fell in love with her.

In February the popular anti-American feeling rose even higher. Two journalists from the United States were thrown out of the country in reprisal for a systematic campaign they had been conducting against the government, which they accused of being a pawn of communism. The Catholic Church was also warned against interfering, and one priest was forced to leave the country.

During those days we took part in an excursion organized by the president's office. The idea of the trip was to show off the Public Health Works that were being finished in Quetzaltenango, where the revolutionary government had already installed a potable water system and a hospital.

Among others on the trip was an American couple, Robert Alexander and his wife. Alexander was a professor of economics at Rutgers University. He and his wife asked questions and wrote down the answers with the passion for order that makes American university professors a different breed from those in other parts of the world. This careful recording of everything that was going on caught Ché's attention, and soon he couldn't take his eyes off Alexander and his notes.

Guevara and I, together with a high-ranking bureaucrat, got

into the front seat of a large station wagon and immediately discovered a machine gun on the floor. Guevara asked what it was for and the bureaucrat answered proudly: "So that we won't be caught like you Argentines, without our weapons. Here they'll have to fight us to the last man, you'll see . . ."

In the combat zone that the Caribbean seemed to be in those days, this kind of bravado made us Argentines feel inhibited and inferior. Some months later I was to ask Guevara what the bureaucrat had done when the time for action came, but at that moment he gave the impression of being a fighter ready to sacrifice his life.

On our return from Quetzaltenango, Guevara might doubt everything he had seen, except one thing: the United States professor who hadn't let a minute go by without writing something in his notebook, he had to be a spy. I expressed my doubts.

"Too many *gringos*, too many *gringos*," was his answer. "What do you think they're doing here? What are they, private investigators, FBI agents?"

It was difficult to be reasonable about this, when every time we stepped into the street we could find agitators in the pay of the CIA. They gathered in the cafés, dropping their voices to ask for details about the political organization and, especially, how much confidence in the revolutionary government the army still had.

The problem of the army was the critical point in the whole process, although the revolutionaries didn't see it this way. Guevara was convinced that in this respect Guatemala's backwardness was much more dangerous than Bolivia's. There we had seen for ourselves a military organization of miners and peasants based, whatever its lack of consolidation, on the fact that the workers had defeated the professional army. The Guatemalan professional army had participated in the government for the past ten years, but would it allow the political revolution to continue now that the United States was officially opposed to it? Guevara didn't think so, and one day we went to question the staff of the revolutionary youth movement about this.

"You have tremendous confidence in the young officers, don't you?" Guevara asked.

"Yes," was the answer, "because they studied under Colonel Arbenz at the Military Academy . . ."

"But do you really believe that their way of life, their family upbringing, everything that sets this group apart socially will resist Yankee pressure, if it turns brutal?"

The young revolutionaries said yes. But Guevara advised them to arm peasant militias like the ones we had seen in Bolivia, but better ones, if possible—militias that not only could keep an eye on the army but, if necessary, could replace it and take over the country's defense.

Guevara's fears were dramatically realized a few months later, but I wasn't there to see it. I left Guatemala at the end of February 1954 for Mexico and the United States, where I was to spend almost a year.

We embraced.

"Wait for me in Mexico," he managed to yell at me as the bus pulled away.

In Guatemala the drama was nearing its final act.

3

The Making of a Revolutionary

"Why not?" Guevara asked with a grin, moving around a modest pine table and pretending, in an exaggerated way, to snap pictures. He was holding a cheap professional camera.

A minute before, after a big abrazo, he had started explaining, with mischief in his eye, how he was earning a living as a photographer in the city's squares and boulevards. The "technical" problem was that the only people in Mexico who could pay for these street photos were the tourists, but most of these were Americans, and an American tourist without a camera was almost inconceivable.

"The potential market," Guevara joked, "is enormous, but the real market, make no bones about it, means slow starvation."

In April 1955, after leaving Guevara in Guatemala and spending a year in the United States, I flew to Mexico to join some friends I had promised to meet there.

I knew Guevara was still alive. He had gotten out of Guatemala at the last minute, and I wanted to see him and hear his personal account of the fall of Arbenz's government.

Guevara occupied a cheap apartment at 40 Nápoles Street.

He lived there with his wife, Hilda Gadea, and their daughter. A third adult shared the apartment, a pint-sized Guatemalan who had also fled the country, joining Guevara on the train to Tapachula, one of the first stops on the way to the capital. This tiny Guatemalan whom everybody called "The Kid" was Guevara's partner in the meager photography business. There was a third associate, a Mexican who provided a lab to develop the plates the other two brought in from the street every day.

That year, in all likelihood during his political asylum in the Argentine Embassy in Guatemala, Guevara had taken up politics, a politics whose path led through revolution. He was thinner, and despite his job as a street photographer he still looked like a university student on vacation.

"Do you remember the guy from the President's office, who carried the machine gun on the floor of his car?" Guevara asked, starting to tell me what had happened in Guatemala after I left.

How could I forget him, the way he had humiliated us with his machine gun and his promise to fight to the death!

"You remember him, right?" Guevara went on. "Well, he was one of the first to clear out," and he let out a horselaugh, filled with the disappointment and contempt he always felt for bluffers.

Guevara had watched the stormclouds boiling over Guatemala, especially after the Tenth Inter-American Conference of Ministers assembled in Caracas in March 1954.

It was common knowledge in Guatemala City, down to minute details, that a mercenary army was being recruited in Tegucigalpa, Honduras. Its members identified themselves publicly with a crucifix transfixed by a dagger. This irregular force consisted of Nicaraguans, Hondurans, and Dominicans who had been hired in their own countries, and a number of Cubans and Colombians who had fought in Korea and were temporarily out of work. A collection of no more than six hundred men, with an additional two hundred Guatemalans, it was not a serious military threat.

Still, it might have an effect on the internal front, which, if not held together on a solid foundation, could easily collapse before the armies had tested each other.

A week before the invasion, airplanes flown by U.S. pilots dropped thousands of leaflets in which people were encouraged to join the "liberating army," then bivouacked on the border. Colonel Castillo Armas thundered his threats over the radio and the government saw its relations with the Catholic Church growing worse. On its part, the Church exaggerated its preoccupation about the leftist character of the regime.

The invasion began on June 18, 1954, at four points on the Honduran border. But it was obvious that the invading contingent could not fight an army of seven thousand, and no one expected a real battle to take place. During the first days the invaders advanced about ten miles without meeting any resistance. Then for a moment it looked as if the Guatemalan army would back its government. There was a clash, and Castillo Armas' irregular troops were virtually scattered.

Guevara had understood at once that the battle would have to be fought in the capital, where the confusion of revolutionary forces might lead to a collapse of the resistance. He set out on a desperate round of calls to convince the organizations of young revolutionaries to take over immediate control of the capital. Guevara had proposed that they first get an iron grip on the city and then isolate the invading force, whose capacity to attack was militarily insignificant. This double operation would doom Castillo Armas' expedition. But to carry it out arms had to be distributed to civil organizations, including numerous parties that professed loyalty to the revolution as well as to union and peasant groups; this outraged the army professional in Arbenz.

Between the 18th and the 25th of June—that is, from the day the invasion began to the moment Arbenz resigned—the capital was a huge stage on which many false heroics were exhibited and unadmitted acts of cowardice came to light. The government's failure to stop the ridiculous mercenary force quickened the collapse of the army's morale. Even before Arbenz abdicated power, civil agents of the Guatemalan Right wing began to prepare the bloody purge that would follow his fall.

At this point, early one morning, the Argentine ambassador called on Guevara at his boarding house.

"Guevara, come with me right away," he told him.

"Why?" he answered. "Nothing's going to happen to me, no one knows me."

"That's what you think," the Ambassador continued. "I've been notified that there's an Argentine on the list of agitators to be executed, and that Argentine is you."

He tried to turn down the protection offered him by the diplomat, but the latter finally convinced him with a simple reflection:

"You can't do by yourself what the government isn't willing to do."

And so Ernesto Guevara saved his own life, remaining for about a month in Peron's embassy in Guatemala. Argentina had to support those who condemned Arbenz's government, and when he fell, the Argentine government obtained permission to take out of the country, aboard military planes, those who had sought asylum in its embassy. Guevara was invited to return to Argentina on one of these flights, but he refused. He asked for a safe-conduct to leave for Mexico.

Now here we were in Mexico. Click, click, and Guevara playfully fired his camera. Then he grew serious again as he and "The Kid" recalled what had broken loose after Arbenz's fall: political purges and assassinations, the revenge of the big landowners, the abolition of the peasant programs, and the everlasting reign of United Fruit.

On the morning of May 1, 1955, Guevara came to my hotel.

"The Mexican revolution is dead; it has been dead a long time, and we hadn't even noticed. Let's go watch the parade of the organized workers. It's like a funeral," he told me.

The parade was in El Zócalo. Long columns of union members wearing steel-blue trousers carried huge signs that identified their organizations and announced their adherence to the politics of the government. At times, we got the feeling that we were watching a parade of workers in a socialist country in Europe. The column was made of nurses and social workers, survivors of the agrarian struggles and other historic movements of the Mexican people. Everyone seemed united behind revolutionary ideals, but watching them, Guevara looked discouraged and remarked rather sadly, "They're united by the state budget, the government payroll. Come on, let's go, *viejo*."

That afternoon Guevara and I ended up at the Monument of the Martyred Youth, which honors the cadets of Chapultepec, who fought to the death against General Pershing's army.

The next day Guevara heard moving news. His Cuban friends, many of whom we had met together in Costa Rica and Guatemala, announced that Batista was having internal and international difficulties and seemed about to approve a law of amnesty. On May 3 the rumor grew. In an apartment in the Imperial building we listened to radio newscasts from Cuba announcing that the senate had approved the amnesty law.

An impressive Cuban colony lived in the Imperial Apartments. Scattered over several floors you could find the founders of the 26th of July, or intellectuals of the opposition, like Raúl Roa, who was then a professed enemy of Communism. This colony, or most of it, lived in expectation of the amnesty law, which would mean the release of Fidel Castro and the veterans of the assault on the Moncada barracks. The Cubans had been gathering in Mexico to wait for him.

Guevara's initial incredulity towards the Cubans had given way to growing enthusiasm. The major reason for this change was that in Guatemala he had permanently lost his assurance that power could be won and kept by peaceful means. Through his contact with the Cubans he had discovered that a large part of the adventures they had related were true. Many among them had died and others had been wounded or taken prisoner.

His bond with the Cubans had sprung up spontaneously, inspired by their youth and the fact that so many of them were university students, as well as by the Cubans' open character, a strong attraction for a man as unconstrained as he. Guevara recognized that doing important things need not deprive one of a sense of humor—that was why the Latin American "doctors," with their strait-laced ways and their incapacity for action, depressed him—and he felt strongly drawn to the raucous Cubans, men capable of firing a potshot at the morning star.

Guevara suggested that if I stopped in Cuba on my way back to the United States, I would be finally convinced of the existence of an active revolutionary element on the island. When I told Roa about this a few days later, at the ranch in Cuernavaca owned by the Venezuelan poet Eloy Blanco, he also thought my visit to Havana was a good idea. A great many Venezuelans used to get together at this ranch, and the idea of bringing down established power by armed force was becoming increasingly attractive to them. Gonzalo Barrios, who later became Secretary of the Interior in Venezuela and tried to crush the guerrilla movement, was then among the minority who upheld the necessity of a "people's war." These were friendly, open reunions, distinguished by the gentle spirit of the host, one of Latin America's finest poets, who died a short time later under tragic circumstances. Guevara enjoyed the company of these men. The passion for politics they all shared created a warm fellowship.

But when I reached Havana on May 7, 1955, the optimism of

the Cuban colony in Mexico seemed a bit excessive to me. The amnesty law had been suspended or Batista had refused to sign it, perhaps because the price he asked was not acceptable to the opposition. I had a letter of recommendation from Roa to a Doctor Martí, asking him to show me the most important things in Cuba at the moment. Evidently Roa's interests differed from Martí's: we went night-club hopping several nights in a row in his late-model car. In the mornings I used to wander alone into the streets around Belascosin Street, where the Hotel San Luis stood. I had ended up staying there on the recommendation of Guevara's Cuban friends. According to them the owner was a fellow-sympathizer, but he seemed to be consumed above all by an absolute hatred for Batista. Sometimes in broad daylight I could hear machine-gun fire which, the hotel owner had explained the first time, came from the university grounds. Generally the volleys were fired from inside the university whenever a patrol car drove by.

Martí, who was also editor of the newspaper *El Mundo,* was skeptical about future political changes on the island.

"Look," he said, pointing to some poor creatures sleeping under the arcades in the sweltering midday heat. "What can *they* possibly want to change? They have no worries, and they're happy, in their own way. Nothing will ever happen in Cuba."

What I saw immediately was that nothing important would happen during the short time I had planned to be in Havana. The amnesty law was apparently stranded on Batista's desk, and a period of patient waiting had set in. I went back to New York with a contradictory double image of Havana in my mind—the luxurious night spots, and the streets crawling with misery in broad daylight.

One afternoon in June 1955, as I was leaving the metal works in the New York suburb where I worked, I found the papers screaming the news that Buenos Aires had been bombed from the air.

There were hundreds of dead. The news hit me so hard that for a moment I felt as if all the blood had drained from my body. There had been a *putsch* against Peron; it had failed but had inflicted a mortal wound on his government. I was Peron's political enemy, a fugitive from his police with a high price on my head, but I saw no reason to be happy about the bombardment. A few days later I received letters from my family giving their own account of what had happened. Naturally, from their point of view Peron's fall and my return to Argentina were more important than an historical appreciation of the events. To my father at his estate in Entre Ríos, the thought that his lawyer son should be making a living as a metal worker in the United States seemed unbearable. He bore it, finally, because he preferred his son to be a common worker in the United States rather than a political prisoner in Argentina.

I had been psychologically prepared for an extended stay in the United States and had become oriented like any other immigrant, although I never thought of making it my permanent home. I had begun by picking tobacco in Hartford, Connecticut, among Negroes from the British West Indies, on the lowest rung of the American proletariat. After that I was a model in an art school on 51st Street and Fifth Avenue, in painting classes for company executives alienated by capitalist society.

In the metal works I had reached the point where I was earning two dollars and seventy cents an hour as a finisher, having started out as a handy-man. I also attended political science courses at the New School for Social Research as well as Professor Frank Tannenbaum's classes on Latin American politics at Columbia University.

From my friend Arturo Frondizi I received a straight account of the events. Since the start of my exile we had kept up a steady correspondence. Guevara and I had read more than one letter from Frondizi, filled with reflections on the future of Argentina;

we had discussed each one and used it as a document for analysis. Guevara had no objections then to what I told him of Frondizi's intellectual personality. Yet he invariably ended up grumbling that while Frondizi would do things better than the others he would not do them differently.

We Argentines living in New York became well known during these months, especially in university circles. Friends from Argentina informed me that in September the armed forces would overthrow Peron's long-lasting government. And, indeed, Peron fell in September. Yet the nature of the regime that took over in Argentina remained imperfectly defined for several weeks, without denying its Right-wing orientation.

Frondizi cabled me that a navy airplane would fly to Mexico to pick up the Argentines scattered through Central America and return them to Buenos Aires. There was room for me on this plane, so I found out when the aircraft would arrive and departed for Mexico. The day I landed at the airport in Mexico City, the newsboys were announcing the fall of General Lonardi, who had overthrown Peron, and the latter's return to the government. I had settled all my personal affairs in New York, and the thought that now there would be no plane arriving to pick me up was disconcerting.

I headed straight for Guevara's place. Naturally, he had been following the march of events in Argentina, and he quickly set me straight on the false report of Peron's return. That night I tried to convince Guevara he ought to go back to Argentina. I even promised to get him a ticket on the naval plane I would be taking—at the moment I didn't even have a ticket for myself, though I had no trouble getting it a few days later from Captain Bassi, the aircraft's commander.

"No, I'm not going. Why should I?" was Guevara's answer. "There's something serious going on here, this Cuba business, which gets bigger every day. What's down there? Right now, a military government trying to reduce the workers' role in the political administration of the country. Let's suppose this new government disappears—one disappeared yesterday—and your friend Frondizi gets in, and you get to be a minister. What can you do? A well-intentioned government with few deep changes, and the day you try to make those changes, zzzip . . . !" Guevara made a slashing motion across his throat.

The airplane from Argentina arrived in Mexico three weeks late because the military regime, with all its internal problems, was keeping a strict count of its resources, and an airplane is an airplane, after all.

During this period I recommended Guevara to a prominent editor in Mexico, Arnaldo Orfila Reynal, an Argentine who directed the Fondo de Cultura Económica publishing house. Guevara had given up photography, and he now carried around a salesman's bag, selling books on time payments. He had a double interest in this. Aside from giving him a living it put in his hands a number of expensive books that he had been reading systematically for some time. The Marxist classics, Lenin's collected works, and texts dealing with the military strategy of the Spanish Civil War passed before Guevara's avid eyes every night. In the morning they were slipped back into the leather bag with which he visited offices and private homes. But nothing positive came of Guevara's meeting with the editor, probably because he automatically raised a barrier of pride whenever he had to ask very powerful persons for anything, and Orfila Reynal was extremely important in Mexico at the time. The personal charm Guevara evinced at friendly gatherings disappeared when he had to ask for anything, and his face took on a serious air of concentration. He wasn't exactly cut out to be a salesman.

Fidel Castro and his brother Raúl were in Mexico. Some time before my latest meeting with Guevara, Fidel Castro had made a tour of several cities in the United States, and I had listened to his followers give a performance which became celebrated in New York. At the end of it lovely girls had collected money in a machine gun made of wood and multicolored paper.

Guevara took me to meet Fidel the second week in November 1955. Castro was now living in a different apartment of the Imperial building. There I ran into Nico López, whom I had met in Guatemala and who would be killed the following year in the *Granma* expedition.

At Castro's place was a crowd of voluble people accustomed to talking in shouts. There weren't enough chairs, and many of them sat and argued on the floor. Large cigars sent up thick clouds of smoke and an aroma that mingled with the odor of sweaty young bodies packed into every room. The noise was so deafening that Guevara took me by the arm and said in my ear, "Come on, let's go shut ourselves in the kitchen. It's the one place where we can talk."

Fidel Castro was in the kitchen boiling a huge pot of spaghetti. The atmosphere of perpetual conspiracy in which the Cubans lived required constant improvisation. Castro kept an eye on the spaghetti and, at Guevara's request, began briefing me on the plans for his expedition.

"We have the ship, the arms, and we have men being readied. We're going to Cuba next year. We'll either be killed or become free men. But right now we have the Mexican police and the Batista spies on our tails. Tell me, are you in good standing with the local police?"

I explained about my having lived with a double safe-conduct for two years, though now I'd have no problem getting a new Argentine passport. Besides, the Mexican authorities knew that an Argentine navy plane would soon be coming to pick up those who wanted to return to Buenos Aires.

"Perfect, it's better that way. We have a feeling they're going to try to put the heat on us, to throw us all in jail for a while. As for our expedition, once our force enters Cuban territory, the work in the cities will begin. Actually, the work is already in progress, our friends are doing it. But the minute we set foot in Cuba, every bomb that explodes in Havana will loosen thousands of tongues, and everyone will be talking about us, about how we fought. You understand, don't you?"

The kitchen door opened and closed every few minutes. Men came in with messages or news just heard over the Havana radio: another criticism of Castro's recent proselytizing in the United States.

Castro answered each question and reclosed the kitchen door with his foot. I asked for details about the expedition he was preparing, and gradually I reached the conclusion that they didn't really have a ship yet to take them to Cuba, although they might have already collected the money to buy one. Nor did they seem to be going through any systematic military training, although they were probably ready to start it very soon. My questions on this point set off an exchange of knowing looks and a reference to the "professor of English." I didn't understand it then, but a long time afterward Guevara explained that the "professor of English" was Colonel Bayo, a Cuban who had done military service in Spain. He saw to the technical preparation of Castro's forces.

The project Castro talked about with such enthusiasm didn't seem very foolproof. There was a lot going against it. They could be successful, but from the way he explained the enterprise, success appeared doubtful. With the passing of the years I've come to the conclusion that the *Granma* expedition of eighty-two men was a success precisely because it had begun with the idea that it *could not* succeed. They broke all the rules regarding navigation, supplies, and military equipment. It was a challenge as one-sided, though on a much smaller scale, as the armed struggle of the Vietcong against the military forces of the United States. Yet when the two entirely different techniques were matched, it was the very weakness of the one, from the other's viewpoint, that allowed it to continue its activity indefinitely. The Cuban army *could not* take seriously the military threat of the small armed force of the 26th of July. In much the same way, the Guatemalan army had not conceded military importance to Castillo Armas' invading band. Both armies lost their war because the solution of the contest was political, not military.

But on this occasion, when Fidel Castro was explaining for the thousandth time how his armed expedition would work, it sounded like science fiction. I told him so:

"Do you know where we in Buenos Aires lock up people with ideas like yours? In Vieytes!"

Guevara laughed, explaining to the others that Vieytes is the popular name for the oldest insane asylum in Argentina.

Right up to the last minute I tried to persuade Guevara to return to Buenos Aires on the navy airplane. We discussed the question, walking the streets of Mexico City from one end to the other. This was Guevara's favorite way of dealing with important decisions. A tireless walker whether in the country or the city, he continually wore holes in his shoes, as could be seen every time he crossed his legs. He didn't care, of course, and this indifference sometimes resulted in amusing moments, such as the time we asked the great exiled Spanish poet, León Felipe, for an interview.

The poet was one of the fifty thousand exiles who then lived in Mexico, among whom the Spaniards still formed the largest group. Guevara had discovered León Felipe's poetry in one of the books he sold for a living, and when he heard that the poet lived right in Mexico City, he asked me if I'd go with him to a Spanish Republican club where we could find him. We went one afternoon, and someone pointed him out to us. He asked us to sit down. He and Guevara sat on a loveseat, and I occupied an arm-

chair facing them. While we were still going through our intro-
ductions, Guevara and the Spanish poet crossed their left legs
over their knees, almost at the same time. I couldn't suppress a discreet smile: they had both exposed the soles of their shoes for a
moment, showing the same gaping wounds.

In 1964, when he was one of the most powerful men in Cuba,
Guevara remembered the old poet and sent him a letter with a
beautiful thought.

"Perhaps you will be interested to know," he wrote to him,
"that one of the two or three books I keep at my bedside is *El
Ciervo* (The Hart). I seldom have a chance to read it because, in
Cuba, sleep or even rest is still a sin of sloth.

"The other day I attended a ceremony that had great signifi-
cance for me. The hall was packed with enthusiastic workers and
there was a sense of the New Man in the air. A drop of the failed
poet I carry in me bubbled to the surface, and I quoted from your
poetry in order to illustrate an argument, at a distance. It's my
homage to you, I beg you to interpret it that way. If you feel
tempted by the challenge to debate about the New Man, the
invitation stands."

But Mexico City, paradise of exiles, so friendly to those recently
arrived, was terribly hard in the long run because of the virtual
prohibition to work that hung over the heads of foreigners. In
that city, where his painful attacks of asthma prostrated him for
hours at a time, Ernesto Guevara burnt all his bridges in favor of
an adventure whose success he was not too sure of, as he himself
admitted after the triumph.

His wife Hilda was contributing to the insignificant family
budget with her salary from a poorly paid office job. And their
daughter, also named Hilda, was growing up in an atmosphere
filled with the hopes and failures of the exiled. It was an atmosphere much too depressing for Guevara. Nor did Castro and his
friends seem cut out for long exile; if there was any doubt in

their minds, the caravan of defeated Spanish emigrés was enough to make them want to return to Cuba.

Guevara's personality took definitive form in Mexico. Some of the scientific preoccupations that had previously guided his actions were relegated to secondary importance, his ideological development reached a high theoretic level, and, thanks to the "professor of English," he received an effective military education.

Guevara's personality had been rounded out in such a way that, undoubtedly, the only field of action left him was the Caribbean. Political action as it might develop in Argentina would have sent him back to a style that had never been his, and was even less so now.

He was repelled by the ways of democratic reform, and what Argentina had to offer him in 1955 was nothing more or less than to bury himself in an ant-heap of small parties and factions, much like the situation in Guatemala and Cuba. His contempt for partisan politics stemmed from a moralistic viewpoint, and Fidel Castro had arrived at this same contempt by the different route of an intense, short experience. This common attitude, forged by different personal and national problems, led Guevara and Castro to scuttle everything that would not serve the cause of armed struggle, and they set themselves the single task of building a small army.

Shortly before the start of his military training under Colonel Bayo we set out on an excursion like those we used to make during our stay in Bolivia. We traveled in a bus to El Bajío, one of the poorest areas in Mexico, where the peasants painfully wrest their crops from the dry ground of the *meseta*, whose hard crust resists life. It was Sunday. On the common outside of Querétaro, the peasants were silently entering a small church. Ernesto Guevara and I followed them in. They were performing a rite of servility, but it was impossible to guess from where they had inherited it, whether from the Spanish colonizers or from the Aztec emperors.

They carried their offerings to the priest—ears of corn, eggs, and chickens—in their hands or in woven baskets. They took off their huge hats, and as they knelt, they pulled up their white trousers, displaying coarse sandals. It was a scene of plastic beauty, but depressing from a historical point of view. These humble Indian peasants gave the impression that time had stopped in El Bajío And we were determined to make time run.

"I would say," Guevara remarked, dusting himself off as if he wanted to brush away the lovely feudal scene, "that the famous Mexican revolution didn't make it." He paused and then concluded, with irony ". . . not very far, anyway."

When we stopped in Querétaro, on the other hand, the immobility of the place was dispelled by a breath of history. There the Mexican insurgents had executed Emperor Maximilian of Austria, thus ending European domination.

"These Indians," Guevara murmured at this historic spot, "would make good fighters. It would only be a question of having time to explain to them how it should be done and who is their enemy, don't you think?"

In December 1955 I left Guevara in Mexico. He had a burning optimism about Castro's undertaking, and he felt authentic friendship toward his Cuban comrades. The adventure interested him politically, but on a human level also. With the Cubans he shared the brotherhood of a large family, and with his personal qualities he had won their common esteem.

He gave me a letter for his mother, Celia, and a few days later in Buenos Aires I handed it to her myself. That's when my friendship with this extraordinary and loyal woman began. It lasted almost ten years, until her death in 1965.

part two

GOVERNING CUBA

part two

GOVERNING CUBA

Historical Background

On March 10, 1952, Colonel Fulgencio Batista, an ex-sergeant backed by the United States, overthrew Cuba's constitutional government and set up a military dictatorship that was to last six years and ten months.

Sixteen months after Batista took over, Fidel Castro, a twenty-six-year-old university student leader from a family of rich land-owners, led the first armed rising against the regime. A hundred young men attacked the Moncada barracks in Santiago. The assault failed, but it laid the foundation for the rebel movement, called the *26th of July* to commemorate the date of the Moncada raid. In October 1953, while in prison, Castro expressed his political aims in a famous statement that went around the island and was converted into a platform, both theoretical and practical, for revolutionary action.

Castro's political philosophy was nationalistic and democratic. It caught on at once among university students all over Cuba and spread quickly to other social elements in the cities, although its limitations were obvious. The Cuban Communists, for example, considered it a movement of middle class radicals, with adventurers and opportunists thrown in, and did not support it at any time. Its social and ideological heterogeneity aroused an understandable sympathy among the veteran politicians of Cuba, all of whom were ready to use the energy and courage of the young for their own interests. The movement's exploits also dazzled Cuban high society, whose sons frequently felt attracted to the rebels and joined their ranks. On the other hand, the vast peasant class remained indifferent to the 26th of July, and outside of the principal cities it had almost no repercussion.

After completing his sentence, Castro left Cuba for Mexico to organize what became his expedition of eighty-two men aboard the yacht *Granma* in November 1956. The ill-fated crossing ended in a hurried landing on the southern coast of the island on December 2nd at a place called Belic, near Sierra Maestra. A uprising in Santiago failed, although it had been prepared by the university student leader Frank Pais to coincide with the landing of the *Granma*.

On December 5th the expeditionary group was attacked by the army and cut to pieces. Ché Guevara, a member of the expedition, would always remember this tragic clash as the day he decided between a medical practice and the revolutionary struggle.

"Perhaps," he wrote, "it was the first time I was clearly faced by the choice between my dedication to medicine and my duty as a revolutionary soldier. There in front of me I had a haversack filled with medications and a box of bullets. The two were too heavy to carry at the same time. I picked up the box, leaving the haversack there, and lit out across the clearing."

On December 18, 1956, the twelve survivors of the landing gathered together and formed the first guerrilla group in Sierra Maestra. During the following month they were joined by five peasants. It was the beginning of the alliance between the young idealistic students from the cities and the long-suffering field hands. Together they attacked the La Plata barracks on January 17, 1957.

On March 13th another organization of rebel students, the Revolutionary Directorate (DIER), attacked the government palace in Havana in an attempt to finish off Batista; they failed, and the bloody repression that followed split Cuban society even more. Many young men migrated from the cities to the country, following the road to Sierra Maestra. Others remained in the cities to organize acts of terrorism. In the next months, the electric works in Havana were dynamited and bombs exploded everywhere. In May Castro's guerrillas captured a garrison in Uvero and seized a large quantity of arms. Batista's reaction was to order the arrest of Frank Pais, the student leader, and subsequently to have him executed. The funeral became a national event, and the people of Santiago poured into the streets to accompany Pais' remains. The local chief of police, afraid of a popular uprising, ordered his men to machine-gun the women and children leading the funeral procession. For three days the city was paralyzed in an act of protest.

Batista's vicious reprisals and the actions of his police only served to turn more segments of the population against him. A part of the navy, joined by members of the 26th of July, attacked and captured the city of Cienfuegos. On the night of November 9, 1957, a hundred bombs exploded in Havana, and the news went out that the first "Free Territory" had been established in El Hombrito, Sierra Maestra. All-out war was now underway.

In March 1958 Raúl Castro, Fidel's younger brother, opened the Second Front in the mountains up north. At the same time Camilo Cienfuegos, a young lieutenant, came down from the hills and harrassed the army with guerrilla tactics, while Juan Almeida led another armed band in an attack on Santiago.

The 26th of July was now a national movement, though it hadn't yet won over the working class. But it had gone far since its beginning in 1953, and peasants swelled its ranks. In the cities, however, the factory workers stayed aloof, and a call for a general strike on April 9, 1958, went unheeded. At this point Batista realized that he would have to use the whole weight of the army to crush the guerrillas, and as soon as possible. The political parties were agitating in the cities, business was falling, tourism was slack, and the big financial interests, both Cuban and American, were beginning to question the dictatorship's real strength. Fourteen army battalions, supported by the air force, the artillery, and the navy, hurled themselves against Castro's guerrillas. In little more than a month the Army occupied 90 per cent of guerrilla territory. Three hundred men under Castro held out against thousands of soldiers.

In July 1958 the guerrillas recovered the initiative, and after eleven days of fighting, two hundred and fifty soldiers surrendered. In addition to this military success Castro gained a notable political victory when nearly all the opposition parties, those of the center and even those of the Right, signed a pact on the 20th, in Caracas, to join forces with him and overthrow the dictatorship. The Communists, who still suspected Castro's motives, abstained.

In August skirmishes broke out everywhere on the island, and the Army's morale disintegrated completely. Differences among the officer corps, particularly between Batista's favorites and the other military, came out in the open.

The dictator called for general elections on November 3, 1958, with the obvious intention of setting up a candidate he could trust and at the same time foisting a "constitutional" succession on the various political parties. However, the elections were boycotted, not just by the 26th of July movement but, as a result of the pact in Caracas, by the other parties also. This repudiation assumed extraordinary proportions. Backed into a corner, Batista resorted to police violence: assassinations increased in the cities, and corpses in the street became a common sight. But there was no way of stopping terrorist bombs right in the middle of Havana's business district.

Batista's political disaster grew in direct proportion to the guerrilla's general offensive. Camilo Cienfugos' column crossed three provinces, reaching the center of the island from the north. In the south Ché Guevara's column reached the Escambray mountains, where it established contact with the guerrillas of the Revolutionary Directorate. One column began the siege of Santiago, and others led by Fidel Castro, Juan Almeida, and Raúl Castro converged on the city.

The decisive battle was the taking of Santa Clara by Ché's column on December 29, 1958. Ché's men also destroyed a military train and took more than a thousand prisoners with arms and munitions. The regime was through.

On December 31st, after twenty-five months of guerrilla war, Batista escaped to Santo Domingo with members of his family and some of his close collaborators. A part of the military brass immediately tried to take over the government, with the blessings of the United States ambassador, but Fidel Castro ordered a general strike and the concentration of all the guerrilla columns on Havana. Santiago, the island's second largest city, surrendered, and a general strike succeeded in paralyzing the attempted coup d'état.

On January 3, 1959, Camilo Cienfuegos and Ché led their men into Havana and took the garrisons of Columbia and La Cabaña, respectively. On the 4th—with Fidel Castro controlling the whole island from Santiago to Havana—Judge Manuel Urrutia was sworn in as provisional President of Cuba. Thousands of soldiers surrendered, thousands of others joined the revolution.

On the 5th, five Latin American countries led by Venezuela recognized the new government. Great Britain and other nations followed suit. The United States finally came around on the 7th, and on the 10th, Ambassador Earl Smith, under heavy pressure from Cuban political opinion which accused him of having backed Batista, was forced to resign.

Castro made his victorious entry into Havana on January 8th.

He announced his government's first measures, among them the withdrawal of the United States' permanent military mission. On the 16th, Washington appointed Philip Bonsal as the new ambassador in Havana. On the same day Fidel Castro assumed the office of prime minister.

From this moment on Washington became increasingly sensitive to the revolutionary government's domestic policies, and Washington's reactions, in turn, became the main catalyst for Cuba's internal changes. The country's long-time economic and political dependence became more evident than ever.

In April 1959 relations seemed to take a friendlier turn when the American Society of Newspaper Editors invited Fidel Castro to visit the United States. Castro had an interview with Vice-President Nixon and Secretary of State Christian Herter, but a vigorous warning about Cuban nationalism and veiled threats against the new government's economic orientation chilled the atmosphere.

On May 2nd, Castro spoke in Buenos Aires before an inter-American committee that was trying to find a remedy for underdevelopment in the hemisphere. He proposed that the United States finance Latin American development with thirty billion dollars. Twenty-four hours hadn't gone by before Under Secretary of State Douglas Dillon answered that the amount was excessive. The Latin American governments thereupon refused to support Fidel Castro's proposal, and he withdrew it.

On May 17th, in Sierra Maestra, the Cuban cabinet passed a law of agrarian reform. It broke up the large landed estates by limiting personal property to a maximum of nine hundred and eighty-eight acres. The American press viewed this as a blow to the individual's right to accumulate wealth, and on Wall Street the stock of the Cuban sugar companies took a sharp dip. Several thousand Americans owned this stock, and its depreciation helped Castro's enemies gain an audience. Foremost among these were Batista's police and military, whom the new Cuban government on its part accused of "war crimes."

In June the Cuban government's first crisis occurred, and five ministers resigned. Ché left on a long tour of Africa and Asia. He had married a Cuban named Aleida March only ten days before, and his precipitous departure was interpreted as the result of pressure put on Castro by those who considered Guevara too far to the left. Ché traveled almost three months, visiting Egypt, Japan, Indonesia, Ceylon, Pakistan, Sudan, Morocco, and Yugoslavia.

However, rightist pressure did not let up with Ché's departure. On June 30th the head of the Cuban air force, Major Díaz Lanz, deserted and fled to the United States. There, at a special session of the Subcommittee of the Senate Internal Security Committee and at a secret meeting with the CIA, he accused the Cuban government of being dominated by Communists. That same day, from his refuge in Santo Domingo, Batista asked Washington for political asylum.

During July rightist opposition to the revolution's reforms increased. On the 18th Castro resigned and publicly accused President Urrutia of obstructing the government's program. There was a general strike in support of Castro, and Urrutia left the government under pressure from the workers and peasants. He was replaced by Osvaldo Dorticós, a lawyer. On the 26th, addressing 600,000 demonstrators, Castro withdraw his resignation. On his right sat the ex-President of Mexico, Lázaro Cárdenas, who had been the leader of Latin America's nationalists ever since his confiscation of the foreign oil companies in 1938.

On August 14th Castro denounced as a farce the Conference of Ministers being held in Santiago, Chile. He also attacked the continual plotting against Cuba by dictator Trujillo from Santo Domingo.

After almost three months' absence, Ché returned to Cuba on September 7, 1959. Castro's position was much more secure now. Undoubtedly, his having kept the most controversial revolutionary leader away from the island while he fought his battle with the Right wing was a political master stroke.

On September 30th Havana announced that it had sold three hundred and thirty thousand tons of sugar to the Soviet Union. The American press asked for immediate economic sanctions against Castro's government, and the surveillance flights over Cuba began.

On October 7th, presiding at a meeting of the National Institute for Agrarian Reform (INRA), Castro announced the appointment of Ché as head of INRA's Department of Industries, although he would still retain his duties in the armed forces.

On October 14th Washington sent an official note to Havana expressing concern for the future of American capital on the island. On October 17th Havana protested to Washington over the State Department's trying to persuade Great Britain not to sell war planes to Cuba.

On October 21st Major Hubert Matos, head of the Camaguey garrison, was implicated in a conspiracy and dismissed from his post. Five hours later bombs rained down on Havana. The American government announced that it would investigate charges that the attack had originated in U.S. territory. Meanwhile, a million people gathered to protest the aggression.

At the end of October President Dorticós made public a conversation he had held with Ambassador Bonsal. The latter had expressed uneasiness about the progress of agrarian reform.

Ché was appointed president of the National Bank of Cuba on November 26th. This decision by the cabinet of ministers put him in charge of virtually all the country's finances.

Throughout the following year the United States continued to show hostility toward Cuba. Three events stood out in 1960. In

January Eisenhower asked Congress for authorization to change U.S. sugar quotas, loading the scales against Cuba. In June the American and British oil refineries refused to purify Russian crude oil and were expropriated by the Cuban government. And in November Havana withdrew from the World Bank.

As President of the National Bank, Ché was the first official to give Cuba's answer to the United States' impending quota restrictions. He affirmed that independence from the United States would now be greater. He also explained that imports would be restricted in order to maintain the country's reserves of foreign currency, and rejecting Ambassador Bonsal's recommendation, he pointed out that Cuba would not take any steps to attract foreign investment, a theme Castro took up and developed some weeks later. This clear-cut anti-capitalistic policy was climaxed by the visit of the Soviety Envoy, Anastas Mikoyan, who arrived in Havana to extend Cuba a $100,000,000 loan at the very moment that Eisenhower passed into law the new sugar quotas. This long-term, low-interest loan had important repercussions on Cuban policy. In the diplomatic sphere, it heralded Cuba's alignment with the socialist nations, consummated at the General Assembly of the United Nations in September. That same month the Havana government established diplomatic relations with the People's Republic of China and North Korea.

On October 21st Ché left the island again, in charge of a commercial delegation. He visited Czechoslovakia, the Soviet Union, and Communist China. In December he signed a commerce agreement with North Korea.

By the end of 1960 there was only one alternative left to Washington and Havana: on January 3, 1961, the two countries broke diplomatic relations.

4

The Eve of Invasion

A boiler about to explode: this was my impression of Cuba the day I landed at Havana's Rancho Boyero Airport in January 1961. Two weeks had passed since President Eisenhower broke off relations with Cuba, and while the Cuban government was placing an unusual degree of confidence in the new President, John F. Kennedy, who would assume office on January 20th, the country still maintained its military appearance. On the highway between the airport and the city I passed one military truck after another and saw soldiers in full combat dress. I had to wonder whether the country really wanted a change.

My first impulse on arriving at the Hotel Nacional was to call Guevara, but I knew he never went to his office at the National Bank until very late in the afternoon, after he had finished with more intense activities, which might be carried out anywhere on the island.

I decided to go for a walk in the streets, now scorching under the midday sun. The wide, treeless paths of the Vedado district seemed to throw off fire, and the glare hurt my eyes. On an avenue near my hotel a detachment of the women's militia marched in military formation with their short machine guns. paratrooper boots, open-necked blouses, and tilted berets.

The image of a country at war could be seen everywhere. I took a ride around the city. There were tents near the docks, and according to the driver of the car, the Via Blanca was mined at its northern end. We drove to Guanabo, a city fifteen miles from Havana, and the chauffeur was forced to make a detour by militia-men perforating the pavement with pneumatic drills preparatory to depositing dynamite charges under the road.

As the chauffeur dodged the pretty girls crossing the street, he recalled the speech Castro had made the day before. Cuba's relations with the United States, the head of the revolution had said, "could get off to a new start with Kennedy." It was an optimistic hope based on the confidence everyone felt in the new President, a man who seemed the very opposite of the ailing general who a few days before had broken off official relations with Cuba.

There was a conspicuous contrast between Castro's moderate tone, calculated to calm the shredded nerves of his people, and the apparent step-up in military activity. Undoubtedly, there were a great many dangers to anticipate. While the greatest menace re-mained an invasion from the sea with American support, there was considerable concern for the increasingly active network of internal saboteurs. On the way back to the hotel the chauffeur brought this danger to my attention, pointing out the bullet scars on a wall. In the quiet Havana nights, while the people took relief from the day's sweltering heat, the shots could be clearly heard. They might come from the Capitol area, a favorite place for surprise attacks on the people's militia, or from the district of the big hotels, to spread alarm among the guests.

I had Guevara's telephone number. It had been given me in

Bonn several weeks before by Jorge Masetti, an Argentine journalist who was Guevara's press correspondent in the West German capital.

I dialed and waited. The voice at the other end was not a secretary's, it was Guevara's.

"The Sniper on an official visit to The Pig," I answered.

He broke up. I had just revived the two names we had used on each other during our wanderings through Latin America. When we first met, Guevara was simply someone thirsty for knowledge of the world. I started calling him the Sniper. But in Mexico, after he considered himself thoroughly committed to the Cuban and Latin American revolution, he affectionately gave me back the nickname. His association with the revolution meant everything, he could no longer be the Sniper. As a boy Guevara had been called The Pig. His teammates on the Atalaya Club rugby team had given him the name, and he accepted it without protesting, in turn coining nicknames for at least six of his friends. The Pig even became his pseudonym in newspaper reports of the team's matches. When we became friends in Bolivia, he said to me:

"Look, Fatso, my friends call me The Pig. They say I make noises when I eat."

Now Ché, The Pig, was the most famous Argentine after Peron.

He wanted to see me right away. He was loaded down with work—his office hours were always at night—but he wanted me to sit in on some audiences, to see a top organism of the revolution in action and observe from within the apparatus that laid down the main lines of Cuba's political economy.

Guevara's office was on an upper floor of a huge, badly finished building, built by the Batista regime to house the Ministry of War. He and his secretaries and assistants occupied a row of large rooms. The personal guard of campaign veterans that accompanied him everywhere rested in one of these half-furnished rooms. The appearance of these bearded men in combat uniform harmonized with Havana's atmosphere of war, but they must have startled more than one foreign official or European banker when they ushered the visitor into their boss's office.

And there he was, standing in his paratrooper's boots, wearing a roomy shirt with its collar turned in, his arms thrown wide. He looked heavier, but later he explained that continual cortisone treatment had given him a moon face.

"It's not fat, no, there's no time for that here," he remarked.

Guevara and I had kept in touch, but we hadn't seen each other since December 1955, when he threw in his lot with the Cuban revolutionaries. Since then Guevara had fought two years in a guerrilla war and had spent another two in the Cuban government. He carried the scars of at least three bullet wounds. He had married again, to a Cuban girl he had met during the war.

"Your story," I told him, "stirs the imagination of young people the world over. The old German officials didn't believe me when I told them how many nights we slept out in the open and had nothing to eat but *plantains*. What can I do to convince them?" I asked, faking a worried tone.

"Do you think they'll believe you if I give you a written statement and we have our picture taken together?" he answered in the same mock-serious tone.

He was exactly the same Guevara I had left five years before. The only difference was a new wholeness to his personality: there wasn't a crack or a seam. This transformation had begun to show clearly during the last days in Mexico. He became methodical and energetic, capable of working without rest whenever the occasion demanded. He had seemed happy in his sloppy ways, but as his ideas became more organized, this disorderliness disappeared. His ideas took shape from the outside world. First he saw the cruelty, the exploitation, and the misery of Latin America. Then he looked for the causes. To conduct his investigation Guevara gave up everything that had previously attracted him.

He discarded Freud's voluminous works and Spengler's theories

on the superiority of the white man. He cut himself off from
everything of European culture that did not serve the liberation
of the Latin American: *mestizo*, Indian, Negro, or white. The
day his intelligence made contact with the reality around him,
he became perfectly tuned, like a well balanced machine. His
creative, quiet capacity for work had found its true outlet, and
Guevara's great conscience was finally at peace. He became a
complete man when the Cuban revolutionaries asked him to
join their cause.

"I expected you about a month ago, *hombre*! I thought I'd find
you here when I came back from my Asian tour. Where have
you been keeping yourself?"

I told him I had resigned from my diplomatic post, with an
extensive written explanation summing up my profound disil-
lusionment with the economic, social, and political conduct of the
Frondizi government, which I had helped to put in power. It was
more than just a bystander's dissatisfaction. I had been morally
compromised, for the government had gone back on the promises
it had made during its electoral campaign, a campaign in which
I had participated.

After leaving the Argentine Embassy in Bonn I had stopped
in New York and was there when relations with Cuba were
broken. Guevara wanted to know how American public opinion
viewed the rupture. I told him the man in the street seemed to
be sincerely convinced that he could expect only the worst
from Cuba, including an armed attack, perhaps a disguised
Soviet aggression. He listened in silence, a huge cigar between
his lips. He made a quick note of something when I told him
about two meetings I'd had in New York, one with Joseph
Newman, a specialist in Latin American affairs for the *New York
Herald Tribune*, and the other with Manuel Ray, an ex-minister
of Castro's government, who claimed to be different from the
other opposition exiles because he defended the social achieve-
ments of the revolution.

I had accompanied Newman on a tour through various provinces of Argentina, shortly before Frondizi became President in 1958. Frondizi had asked me to show him whatever he wanted to see, and we travelled together for several days. Now, during my stop in New York, I remembered Newman and went to look him up at his newspaper. When he found out I was going to Cuba, he questioned me exhaustively on the situation there, a subject on which I could only conjecture from a distance. He wanted to know if Castro was backed by his people, and whether there was any chance of a popular uprising in the event that an expeditionary force repeated Castro's feat and invaded the island. Newman himself had made a tour of the Cuban interior a short time before, and he didn't think an uprising was possible. He gave me the impression that he might be conducting a poll among Latin Americans for someone in a high governmental post. I later learned that Newman was Arthur Schlesinger Jr.'s informant, and his negative opinion on the prospects for an invasion had reached Kennedy, though without affecting the final decision to attack.

Guevara squinted, a way he had of showing curiosity, and said·

"And you, Fatso, what did you answer the *gringo* Newman?"

I had told Newman that I hadn't been to Cuba yet, but that he had been in Argentina in 1945 when Ambassador Braden and the State Department had blockaded Peron. I told Guevara that I had asked Newman, "Do you think that the Argentines would have cooperated with an American invasion at the time?" Newman had shaken his head.

I also gave Guevara my impression of Manuel Ray, a good-natured engineer who insisted that the United States was not opposed to Castro because of his economic and social actions but because of his ties with the Soviet Union. Starting with this premise Ray held that it would be possible to continue the revolution with Castro removed.

"This guy Ray!" Guevara said, rising to his feet. "You can't tell whether he's a sweet little angel or a son of a bitch, or some mixture of both."

Guevara was convinced that despite the change of government in the United States, preparations for an invasion were still underway. Havana had details about these preparations, especially about what was happening on plantations in Guatemala. The problem, therefore, was to know how far Kennedy could go, or wanted to go, to stop these forces. Guevara thought Cuba ought to encourage a change in the United States' determination to launch an invasion, but he felt this change was historically impossible.

"It would be like acknowledging that Betancourt was right, don't you see? That there's a good United States and a bad United States, and that Latin America's fate depends on which of the two is in control. The economic interests are important, but the country itself is a solid block as long as the working class doesn't become conscious of itself as a class and the colored people don't organize a rebellion. But that's still a long way off, eh?"

The entire Cuban government lived with a double prospect— under Kennedy, relations with the United States might improve and even become acceptable; or, on the other hand, the island might be invaded.

For the moment the Cubans had decided to demonstrate again their readiness to reach an understanding. They were transferring entire militia units to work in the fields, playing up the move with lots of publicity so that its political implications should not be lost.

On January 23, 1961, Guevara invited me to travel with him to Cabañas, a small town about twelve miles west of the capital. He came by the Hotel Nacional very early in the morning, as this was the only time of the day you could travel without suffering the full brunt of the tropic heat. Manresa, his secretary and right-hand man, arrived with him. A simple man, courteous without being obsequious, Manresa was the archtype of the man Guevara liked to have around him. He had been a soldier in Batista's army, but Guevara trusted him completely, keeping him informed of a great deal of government business.

The people of Cabañas were gathered in the main square to welcome the militia. A crowd of peasants were singing revolutionary songs, waving their straw hats and encouraging the militiamen, peasants like themselves, who had learned to handle firearms and were returning to work in the cane fields.

Guevara was unusually cautious in the speech he gave shortly before noon. He warned that Kennedy had not yet hinted what his policy toward Cuba would be, and for the moment it was best to put the men back on productive labor.

"If the new administration threatens us," he added, "we shall all be ready to go back to the trenches."

The crowd's reaction seemed ambivalent. Their faces relaxed when the speaker suggested better relations with the United States, but they became set, with an expression of readiness, when he spoke of going back to the trenches. The Cubans didn't want war, but neither were they afraid of it.

Guevara and I got into the habit of meeting every night in his office around twelve o'clock. From that hour until five o'clock A.M. Guevara received visitors. In an adjoining room, where his wife Aleida often attended guests, there was a sack of *yerba mate* and the utensils to prepare it. It was an old River Plate custom he preserved intact. Intimate friends knew that there was no better gift to Ché. The word had spread, and soon there wasn't a university, political, or worker delegation from Argentina, Uruguay, or Paraguay that didn't bring its modest offering of *yerba mate*.

The *mate* was handed around until the sky outside was already growing light. The Argentines in Cuba used to come to Ché's place to celebrate this gauchos' ritual. That's where I finally met Alberto Granados, the biochemist who accompanied Guevara on his first trip outside Argentina when Ché was still a medical student. Granados worked on his specialty in Cuba, and his devotion toward Ché was fully returned.

The idea that Guevara was not a very affectionate person, that it was difficult to make friends with him, or, rather, that his concentration on politics and revolution kept him from fulfilling obligations of friendship, is false. With Granados, Masetti, Gustavo Roca, with me, and with those who were friends at various periods in his life, especially with those who had been close to him before he became famous and powerful, Guevara was an exemplary friend, warm and interested in the problems of others, often to the point of completely forgetting his own importance.

At the end of January Kennedy made a speech on the infiltration of Communism in the nationalist revolutions in Latin America. It was interpreted as a statement addressed specifically to Cuba, and, needless to say, was not favorably received. Moreover, it coincided with the stepped-up activities of saboteurs who, it was proved in some instances, came from American territory. These saboteurs were concentrated in a mountainous region, low, thickly protected by vegetation, and easy to reach by air: Sierra del Escambray.

The American press spoke of a real army, with thousands of well-equipped men waiting for the moment to make their move. Guevara had a much more realistic idea. According to him the band of insurgents numbered no more than two hundred, a size that still justified the Cuban government's concern. At night camouflaged planes dropped big packages with Garand rifles, Browning automatics, and cases of grenades and bazookas that often went directly into the government's arsenals.

The presence of anti-Castro forces could not threaten the government's stability, but as had occurred in 1957 and 1958 they did breed sabotage and agitation in the cities. Several persons were shot by the government. Employees of Havana's electric works who had blown up part of the installations were executed. And awaiting trial were a number of Americans who had been captured while trying to work their way into the island's interior. This situation, exceedingly difficult for the United States to explain, increased the conviction of the Cuban leaders that American spy networks were pursuing plans for an invasion, whatever Kennedy might say to the contrary.

The Cuban government decided to clean out the Escambray mountains with a vast operation in which close to fifteen thousand militia would take part. It was a dangerous task, not because of the enemy's strength, but because of the inexperience of the militia, which until then had engaged only in military exercises. Most of them had had no actual combat experience.

Nevertheless, I accepted enthusiastically Guevara's invitation to join one of the combat units. In the city of Santa Clara, where he wanted me to go, he had fought one of the bloodiest battles in the war against Batista. He had taken more than a thousand prisoners, seized a military train, and captured the city. Santa Clara is the hub of the island's central plain, an important center for railway communications, with a population of over one hundred and fifty thousand.

Guevara recalled a soldier in that battle, an anonymous fighter of the revolution. He had found him sleeping. The soldier had explained that he didn't have a weapon. It had been taken away from him because he had been careless with it. Guevara had told him: "Earn yourself another gun in the front lines. Go there without a gun and come back with one, if you can."

Later, in Santa Clara, Guevara was summoned to a dying soldier's bedside in an improvised hospital.

"Do you remember, Major?" the man said. "You sent me to look for a gun, and I earned it here."

It was a heroic story that always stirred Guevara.

The memory of Guevara's exploits in Santa Clara was still fresh. The walls of the power station and the university buildings still showed bullet marks, and very near the place where the first Catholic Mass in America was celebrated stood the railroad where Ché's men had seized the armored train.

The militias consisted mainly of peasants—simple, open men, like all the peasants we had met in our jaunts through Latin America, but more communicative. They laughed easily and made jokes about their automatic weapons, whose parts gleamed in the midday sun. Many were Negroes, like the young volunteer teacher whom the anti-Castristas in the mountains had recently hanged. It had been a vicious, unpolitical crime following a mock trail at which he had been condemned as a "Communist." The Negro militiamen felt that they must avenge this blood-brother whose mission had been to educate other peasants such as themselves. There wasn't any hatred in them; there was only that degree of anger which Guevara considered absolutely necessary if the revolution was to be invulnerable. These men understood that their freedom was in the mouths of their rifles. As long as they had these, Cuba's sovereignty and their own individual dignity were secure; the two were inseparable.

"Just think," Guevara said to me when I reported my impression. "If Guatemalan peasants had been enlightened in time, neither Castillo Armas nor anybody else, not even the Yankees, would have stopped the agrarian revolution."

For Guevara, a revolutionary's military training was never finished. He had decided he should learn how to pilot a plane, and he had succeeded rapidly. He flew a twin-motored Cessna, previously Castro's, and on some of his trips out of the country he even took the pilot's seat in the huge Britannias.

I traveled from one end of the island to the other in Guevara's plane. It was a curious and revealing experience. Whenever his plane appeared over canefields in the daytime, the fieldhands would stop their work. Lieutenant Eliseo de la Campa, Guevara's personal pilot who took me over the entire island, explained that the peasants knew that either Fidel Castro or Ché was in the plane. When they recognized it in the sky, they would rest their machetes and wave their arms.

Guevara asked the pilot to "take good care" of me. "He's an old friend, see?" He winked, adding, "They may mistake him for a counter-revolutionary and blast you both out of the sky."

The warnings was not altogether frivolous; recently the anti-aircraft artillery had brought down one of their own planes near Veradero Beach. Three of its occupants had died; two of them were in the military, and the other was one of the Party's leaders. The mixup had upset Guevara very much, and at the men's funeral he had said:

"The three were victims of the enemy, because it's the enemy who makes us see phantoms where there aren't any."

He was particularly worried about what he called an invasion psychosis, a state of mind entirely different from preparedness against invasion. During those days he spoke on the subject to various audiences. He couldn't forget the destructive fear that had gripped the Guatemalan people in 1954 and left them practically helpless before the advance of a ridiculous armed force.

Moreover, he saw a relation between invasion hysteria and the recent drop in production. This matter was uppermost in his mind.

"If we continue one more year on the verge of war," he said, "we'll be left without any production at all, and we can't let that happen."

One night he asked me to accompany him at dawn on a

surprise visit to a metal works. These visits were intended to see
how the work was going and therefore had to take place without
warning. At four-thirty the following morning an old Pontiac
came up the automobile ramp at the Hotel Nacional. The
concierge startled me awake.

"Major Guevara and his escort are waiting for you," he
announced.

At that moment no fewer than a hundred young students from
the provinces, in Havana to complete a training course, were on
their way downstairs. We all reached the ground floor at the
same time. Guevara was waiting.

Seeing Ché had a tremendous effect on them; there he was in
flesh and blood, his blouse faded from constant use, his boots
unpolished, and wearing the look of a young boy about to start
on an outing, the same look they had on their own faces.

Ché always aroused respectful curiosity. Whenever he appeared, it was generally realized that this man, born at the far
end of the hemisphere, was working among them because the
Cuban revolution was part of a greater revolution in which
everyone had a role. As we left, the almost magical air of the
young revolutionaries seemed to float around us.

Guevara took the wheel, and his four companions squeezed
into the back seat. I sat next to him as the others settled their
FAL machine guns between their legs, and one lit a cigar he
had let go out. These men of the people, there to protect Guevara
from any terrorist attack, had followed him from Sierra Maestra
to Las Villas, fighting under his orders in the Ciro Redondo
column. They represented the most radical contingent of the
rebel army. This seemed to be the result of their open veneration
for Ché rather than any personal ideology.

Guevara also lit a cigar and invited me to do the same, indicating a handsome box of polished wood sitting between us. When
I raised the lid, I couldn't stifle an exclamation: there were no

cigars in the box. Instead, a dozen hand grenades in a neat row, with their safety pins lined up. I threw him a questioning look because, in addition to the weapons the four men in the back seat were carrying, Guevara had a .45 pistol in his cartridge pouch, suspended from a wide belt woven with fishline.

"What's wrong?" I inquired.

"These are what we use here. A revolutionary's life is hard, it's always hanging from a thread. There are gangs of saboteurs, trained by the CIA, looking to assassinate the heads of the revolution. In case of attack there's no better weapon than a hand grenade aimed well, precisely placed in the middle of the group. Better still, if your nerves are strong enough and you can hold on to it several seconds after pulling the safety pin, the effect can be devastating."

And he immediately took a real cigar out of his upper shirt pocket and handed it to me.

At the metal works Guevara at once went to the manager's office and asked for the attendance list. He discovered that twenty-five per cent of the workers had reported themselves absent, for various reasons: illness, guard duty, political indoctrination. He then requested that the workers present be assembled in the back yard of the plant.

"You can only produce more by work and sacrifice," he told them. "It's easier to die fighting in the trenches than to work three hundred and sixty-five days a year."

Guevara tried to make it clear that Cuba's national production was now in the hands of the proletariat:

"This is a historical moment for the Cuban working class, as well as the working class of all the Americas," he stated, "because everything that's happening in Cuba in these revolutionary times will soon have a repercussion in other countries. Here in Cuba a battle is being fought for the entire future of America, and each time we act and move a step forward, our revolutionary action is helping all of America to break a terrible yoke, one we ourselves are all too familiar with."

On our return to Havana, sometime past midday, Guevara said he was worried about the irregularity in production, which was more acute because of the threat of an attack from outside the country, but which had actually originated in a mistaken interpretation of the control the proletariat should exercise over industry.

The car stopped at a traffic light, and Guevara looked absent-mindedly at the driver of a car braked alongside ours. The man looked back at him with ill-concealed venom, his eyes glaring. Guevara turned toward me with a contented smile.

"Look," he said, "this guy belongs to the middle class, which Fidel still thinks he can count on. Watch his eyes."

But the light had changed and we were moving on.

One night I discovered Guevara had a large map of Argentina in his private bathroom next to his office. It was one of those oilcloth maps the cartographer Bemporat made by the thousands. They're in every school in Argentina. It was a rare find in a bathroom in Havana. I asked him if this wasn't a strange decoration for a toilet.

"You know," he told me, "I'm in the habit of thinking while I sit there. I think about Argentina, its unexploited economic potential, and what the Latin American revolution could gain if it won a point of support and expansion there instead of depending exclusively on a small country like Cuba."

It was a theme that was always on his mind. Guevara was convinced that the Latin American revolution could not expand as long as it didn't have a political and economic bulwark it could count on. Sometimes he also thought about Brazil. The recent rise to power of Janio Quadros, a friend of the Cuban revolution and a visitor to the island, fueled the hope that Brazil would be the country called on to play the decisive role in the liberation of Latin America.

The references to Argentina became more frequent after a completely unexpected incident, one that brought new and interesting participants into the discussions.

One evening as I was getting ready to go to dinner with some friends at the Potin restaurant in Vedado, I received a phone call. The person who was calling had informed the operator that he didn't know me, but that it was urgent that he speak to me.

The stranger turned out to be Angel Borlenghi, the number-two man in Peron's government and his Secretary of the Interior for more than eight years. Borlenghi may not have known me, but I knew him—it was he who had set a price on my head after my escape from prison in Buenos Aires.

Borlenghi wanted to see me right away. I told him I had a dinner date. He kept insisting and I kept saying no, until he finally said in a very subdued voice:

"The thing is, I'm a prisoner right now. I'm at the Malecon police station, the one behind the American Embassy."

The formerly all-powerful minister who had had me jailed for defending political and union prisoners now found himself in the same predicament as my old clients.

When I arrived at the station, the police lieutenant explained Borlenghi's crime. He had not reported his ownership of two houses, something expressly punishable under the new urban reform laws. Again and again Borlenghi made the point that he had the houses not for purposes of real estate speculation, but because an old family situation forced him to keep both at the same time.

When I realized there was no other way to get Peron's ex-minister out of jail I asked for a telephone and called Guevara. I told him the details of the case, and he asked to speak to the police lieutenant. Guevara began by congratulating the policeman for his zeal in seeing the revolutionary laws carried out. He then said he should pursue the case against Borlenghi through the regular judicial channels but should let him go free for now. The lieutenant accepted his proposal, and in no time the Argentine ex-minister was out in the streets.

Some days later Borlenghi asked me if he could thank Guevara personally for his intervention. Guevara accepted, and one night the three of us sat down in the leather armchairs in Guevara's office to drink *mate* and talk about politics.

"There's no question about it, Peron was the most advanced embodiment of political and economic reform in Argentina," Guevara stated. "But look, if he had had a marked effect on the traditional economic establishment, they wouldn't have found themselves in such a good position to overthrow his government."

Borlenghi replied that the forces of gradual development in Argentina allowed for continual growth without having to upset completely the structure of society. As far as he was concerned, the system of distributive justice Peron had established was more than enough to justify his government in the eyes of history. He confessed that he found the speed of the Cuban revolution a dizzying experience. Several times during the conversation Borlenghi came back to the same kind of argument:

"That's fine, that's fine, but when I directed the Union of Mercantile Workers, all we had for our meetings was one room, and during the Peron era it came to be the most powerful organized union in Latin America, with widespread social services and thousands of employees and technicians in its ranks."

Guevara could never get across to Borlenghi, who in his youth had been a social-democrat in the German style, the difference between a reformist, distributive unionism and a unionism based on the idea that the working class should run the nation.

It was in Guevara's offices that I met another of Peron's close collaborators, ex-Chancellor Jeronimo Remorino. He was in Cuba trying to persuade the government to purchase an industrial fertilizer plant in France. A French company had hired Remorino to make the deal. Guevara and Remorino discussed Latin American and United States politics for hours on end. Remorino wanted to know how much loyalty Cuba could reasonably expect of the Soviet Union in the event that her dispute with the United States went too far.

"They could barter Cuba for Berlin or Taiwan," Remorino argued, "for any of their pending problems. The Russians have a national policy, they have permanent interests. At present what they fear most seems to be foreign claims, perhaps because they foresee internal pressure in the United States leading to an aggressive policy, a 'fascism,' American-style, from which it would only be a short step to a general war."

"It couldn't be," Guevara answered, "because this implies that a Communist nation is guided by the same ethics as a capitalist nation, and this is a rejection of the very basis of Communism. Communism is an ethic, an international ethic, not a method of economic development, of distributing incomes and materialistic gains. We in Cuba are convinced that the Soviets will honor socialist solidarity."

To argue with him on this point was like arguing inside the lion's mouth. All you had to do was look out any window, and there, outlined against the horizon, you could see the black shadow of an American cruiser, menacing and silent, armed evidence of the displeasure the world's greatest power felt for the socialist revolution of a small Caribbean island.

Remorino's own political experience was completely different from Borlenghi's, and the fact that both of these men had been in Peron's government proved the variety of Peron's political support. Borlenghi was a unionist, a laborite in the German or

English manner. Remorino was above all a nationalist, in the style of the great European heads of state. De Gaulle was his favorite model.

Yet both these men were equally moved by the seriousness of the Cuban revolution and Guevara's integrity. They were impressed in different ways.

Guevara's contempt for money won Remorino's admiration, for it was a contempt guided by moral and ethical considerations. It reached its highest manifestation the day he signed the Cuban bank notes with his war name, Ché. Guevara knew that with this act he was striking a blow against the philosophy that puts money above everything, investing it with sacramental respect. To break down this myth, to restore the true nature of money as a means of simplifying the exchange of actual goods, was Guevara's intention. The wealthy people in Cuba had stopped hoarding their wealth. When they discovered that it was only printed paper and could no longer be used to purchase more than the necessities of life, or beyond their contribution to the community, they poured it by the millions onto the gaming tables in the casinos. The day he signed Ché on the bills, Guevara had literally knocked the props from under the widespread belief that money was sacred. And around the gaming tables of the Capri, which George Raft had put up several years before, you could see men and women devoured by a secret fever, throwing down on the green baize the banknotes the revolution had compromised forever.

Borlenghi, on the other hand, had been won by Guevara's Jacobin ethics. A change came into his voice when he recalled how Guevara had dealt with a fellow named Schwarzmann, an impresario of obscene shows and a naturalized Argentine, to top it off. Thanks to the British novelist Graham Greene, this man was a part of world literature, for he was none other than the impresario of that notorious little theater in Havana's Chinatown, the Shanghai. In *Our Man in Havana,* Greene described the obscene entertainment at the Shanghai: the show opened with a Negro giant in a performance calculated to appeal to the lowest tastes, and then continued on smaller stages with violations of domestic animals and indescribably perverted and sadistic acts. Guevara had given Schwarzmann a warning, but the man thought he was dealing with an ordinary official, maybe a little cleverer than most, and continued putting on his shows. He was somewhat surprised to have Guevara summon him to headquarters at La Cabaña fortress one day and tell him that he would be tried for the corruption of public morals and probably sentenced to death. For several weeks the Argentine ambassador did his best with Guevara, and although he couldn't get him to admit that Schwarzmann's crime did not deserve capital punishment, he finally made him see that he could not apply the death penalty to a foreigner.

Guevara was completely intransigent about greed. He had sought a society in which each person earned his bread through his own work, giving the best in him. He had hiked through Latin America with nothing but the clothing he wore, taking any job he could get and receiving for his work just enough to live on. It was hard to believe, but he desired nothing else. He had a communal spirit that was both primitive and Christian. To share with others what he earned by work was to him the most natural thing in the world.

A fabulous trove of jewels, precious stones, works of art, ivories, and gold bars had recently been found in the showplace house of a Spanish countess.

"You ought to take a look at it," Guevara told me one day. "You should see what crazy lengths the rich go to."

He gave me a free pass, with his signature. The spectacle was straight out of The Arabian Nights. The two-story mansion of Countess Revilla de Camargo had once been slept in by King

Leopold of Belgium and Don Juan, the Spanish pretender. Now there was a work gang slowly razing a thick wall. Behind it was the greatest pile of riches I've ever seen in my life, outside of museums. Cases of fine porcelains were removed, candelabra and silver services, as well as paintings by Goya and Murillo, carefully crated. The Countess had had an income of three hundred million dollars, produced by sugar and saw mills. At the age of eighty she had decided to emigrate from Cuba, and the day she learned that her properties had been confiscated, she took to bed and shortly died in a clinic for millionaires in New York.

The rich countess, who could not survive the loss of her effortless wealth, had her opposite in the ideal man Guevara wanted to forge in Cuba and throughout Latin America. To achieve this New Man Guevara assigned a vital role to youth and the party organizations.

"Youth is the more important, it's malleable, like clay. With it the New Man can be formed, without inherited weaknesses or cultural and social residues," Guevara explained. He worried about finding a new, enticing way to put into practice his thesis of the New Man:

"Work, with the incorporation of youth, is basic. Work is a prize in certain cases, an instrument of education in others, but never a punishment. With the new generation there will be born a total revision of the concept of work."

Guevara practised his philosophy of work. I had a chance to witness this personally.

One night he warned me:

"Get to bed early tonight. Tomorrow you'll find out what hard work means."

At five o'clock he stopped by the hotel, and we immediately left to join a crowd forming in Plaza de la Revolución. At that hour of the morning there were no fewer than three thousand people waiting for buses and trucks. There were Cuban flags and straw hats everywhere, and the women wore military uniforms or cool, bright clothes. These were the personnel from several government offices, including the National Bank and government planning offices that would shortly be grouped into the Ministry of Industries, under Guevara's leadership.

The surprise Guevara had in store was that this time he would be joined in his volunteer work on the sugar crops by two friends from "the old days," Doctor Granados and me, as well as his wife, Aleida.

I must confess that as we rode the twenty-four miles to the cane fields, I thought the outing would follow a typical Latin American pattern: a minister or a president working in the sun, photographers doing a good job, a backdrop of authentic laborers at work, and the government man with a cool drink in the shade talking about the latest news, surrounded by officials and newsmen. It wasn't that I didn't trust Guevara. Far from that, it was my own incapacity to imagine a situation different from the well-known pattern.

We arrived at last. The trucks were parked together on one side of the road, and the machetes for cutting cane—the famous *mochas* the peasants jubilantly raise high at popular assemblies— were passed around. I received mine, and in an effort to do the job right announced that I'd work without gloves or a shirt.

"I can see you've never done this kind of work," Guevara slowly remarked. He was as smugly pleased as a kid waiting for his cocksure buddy to make an ass of himself. And that's what happened: I didn't know that sugar cane throws off a microscopic powder that enters the pores and irritates and cracks the skin. After a short while I too asked for a long-sleeved shirt and elbow-length gloves.

We worked without stopping from six-thirty A.M. to eleven-thirty A.M. By then the sun made work unbearable, and everyone took time out for lunch under an open shed. There was a general feeling of camaraderie, despite the fact that department heads and ministerial leaders sat together with simple secretaries and workers in the lowest echelons. Guevara was beaming. His ideal seemed to have been achieved. A community of men and women drawn together by work, capable of performing it in a responsible manner, happily gathered together without false respect or sham differences.

The work continued at the same pace from three o'clock to seven-thirty P.M. Guevara was expert at cutting the sugar cane at its base and trimming it with clean machete strokes. When the day's work was over, he climbed into a wagon with enormous wheels, the kind used to carry cane to the factory, and gave us all a doctrinal talk. This quickly turned into a question-and-answer session. The content and direction of the questions gave an idea of how far the political orientation had progressed. Guevara told me afterward that these dialogues, whose subjects were always extemporaneous, raised without any inhibitions, had proved the best gauge of what were really the deepest hopes and fears of the Cuban people. The questions that afternoon naturally centered on the threat of invasion, and no one showed any surprise when Guevara interrupted the dialogue to say:

"And now, friends, let's see how good everyone's eyesight is."

There were peals of laughter, and several people lined up next to Guevara and took out their .45 caliber pistols for target practice on a row of bottles.

At the end of February 1961 Guevara was appointed Minister of Industries in a cabinet shakeup ordered by Castro. In effect, Guevara retained all of his former duties, though now under one ministerial post. He was given plenary powers over all industries in the hope that he would be able to unify, orient, direct, and execute the various plans for industrial development.

He was also put in charge of petroleum exploitation, ore deposits, and the industrial development section of the department in charge of agrarian reform.

The wide powers granted to Guevara were an admission by the government of the need to concentrate in a single head the complex process of industrial expansion which had hitherto been hurt by lack of strict planning. And the fact that Guevara was chosen for the post showed the preference to have someone like him in charge, a man indifferent to demagogy.

Integrating into the country's industrial structure more than sixty new factories obtained from Japan in a barter-trade sugar deal was one of the biggest problems he had to face. Cuba had to "digest" the industrial machinery it had accumulated over two years of revolution before it could put into effect Castro's promise to emancipate the country from agriculture, especially its single-crop economy of sugar.

Guevara was convinced that moral incentives to productivity were a prerequisite for any rational program of industrialization. Accordingly, he made his initial public appearance as Minister to award the government's first prizes for "Heroes of Labor." He used the occasion to announce a four-year plan, calling on hundreds and thousands of new "Heroes of Labor" to help carry it out.

To the American press Guevara's appointment as Minister meant that executive power was rapidly slipping into his hands. At that time Havana was making efforts to halt the deterioration of her relations with other Latin American governments, and the American press so twisted their interpretation of Guevara's appointment that the diplomatic negotiations were severely compromised. Since Guevara stood for the radicalization of the revolution, his enemies seized this moment to exaggerate his importance and thereby created a climate unfavorable to co-operation.

Apparently some thought that it was time to get rid of Guevara. The day he was to be sworn in as Minister, there was an intense fusilade at the intersection of Seventh Avenue and Eighteenth Street in the Miramar district, less than a hundred yards from Guevara's house. The news was not broadcast in Cuba itself, but was heatedly discussed among Guevara's assistants. Guevara told his close friends that it was not an attempt on his life, but after I saw how close to his house it had occurred, I kept thinking for days about the box of grenades he always carried in his car.

In fact, the whole month of March was one long crescendo of violence. There were bursts of machine-gun fire day and night, and time-bombs exploded in the big hotels. It was no secret that an invasion was still on, and the spy agencies of the United States increased their efforts to train saboteurs and land them along the island's extensive coast.

It was at this moment that two reformist presidents, Arturo Frondizi of Argentina and Janio Quadros of Brazil, tried to mediate between the United States and Cuba. Cloaked in diplomatic language, the mediators' premise was that a war over Cuba was unlikely because of the coexistence pact between the United States and Russia. Consequently, there would have to be negotiations, and in this case why not entrust them to the two big brothers in Latin America? Frondizi, who presented the proposal after consultation with Quadros, implied that Washington ought to accept the mediation of two nations in the Western Hemisphere instead of dealing directly with Russia. But Frondizi was wrong in this as well as many other things, and the fruit of his initiative was a bitter campaign against him, not only by Cuban exiles, but also by the Right wing in Argentina and other Latin American countries. The day he tried to intervene in the Cuban question, Frondizi sawed off half the limb he was sitting on.

"He won't have any luck, you'll see," Guevara told me one

night. "And that's not all, he's also giving the reactionaries in Buenos Aires a chance to topple his government."

Diplomatic problems took up as much of Guevara's time as did his Ministry of Industries. Because I was soon to return to the Argentine Embassy in Bonn, where I had been stationed for two years I was asked to elaborate an extensive memorandum for him on Cuban relations with Western Germany.

These relations had been poisoned by something that might almost be considered a Cuban domestic problem. The German commercial attaché in Havana had rented a piece of property confiscated by the government, under a lease with the former owner which had been predated to make it look as if it had been drawn up before the government's confiscation had gone into effect. Perhaps the German diplomat was trying to help out the former owner, now in exile, or perhaps he was profiteering by paying a very low rent, which the other received in dollars. Whatever his reason, when the fiscal seal confirming the expropriation was placed on the building, the diplomat broke it, and hours later the district militia invaded the house.

The German ambassador was Count Karl von Spreti. He believed private property was sacred and literally became ill at the mention of agrarian reform. The Cubans expected that the German government, yielding to pressure from Washington, would break off relations with Cuba. In that expectation, they preferred to take the initiative and break with Bonn first. To test the Germans they decided expel the German attaché.

I had written to Guevara about a curious incident I had been involved in months before, when the Colombian Embassy organized an act of homage from the Latin American diplomats to Chancellor Konrad Adenauer. A Colombian came to the Argentine Embassy with an invitation and discreetly gave me the news that only the Cubans were excluded from the ceremony. In that case, I told him, he could count me out.

Two days later I was surprised when the German Director of

Latin American Affairs informed me that they knew all about the incident. What's more, they shared my position, and not only they but Adenauer himself would refuse the homage if a single diplomatic representative from Latin America were absent. The celebration took place with everyone present, and the old statesman capped his lesson by breaking protocol and addressing the Cuban ambassador first.

Nevertheless, relations with Western Germany were on the downgrade, beyond the point of return. Before March was over, Cuba received a commercial delegation from East Germany and gave it the category of a diplomatic mission, which brought out a new protest from the German count. Relations would be broken off entirely a short time later.

Guevara's first important outing as Minister of Industries was also the last tour of the island we made together. He wanted to see for himself the oil prospecting in Jatibonico, in the province of Camaguey. We went there in a long column of cars, hoping that all those cars of the same make would possibly cut down the risk of assassination in case of a terrorist attack.

"Until now," Guevara explained on the highway, "Shell, Esso, and Texaco, all of which belong to our American friends, had set up only refineries in Cuba. They brought the oil from Venezuela, refined it here, and sold it throughout the Caribbean. When we took over the government, our own oil didn't amount to one per cent of the national consumption. That's why we're so busy looking for it now. I don't like to prophesy, but oil will occupy an important place in Cuba's total economy."

"Wouldn't it be more convenient," I ventured, "to buy it from another producer instead of undertaking the huge expense of exploiting it yourselves?"

"Don't you know what happened? When the Yankees blackmailed us and stopped oil delivery, we turned to Venezuela and Argentina. And do you know what Frondizi answered? What

Betancourt proposed? Almost nothing. That we form joint study committees to decide how to carry out the sale of the oil. A question of months, at a time when we had to have the oil in a matter of hours. A stab in the back that necessarily put us in the hands of the Soviets."

Some days later Guevara took me to the airport in his car. There were machine-gun emplacements along the highway and anti-aircraft guns in the storage areas of the airport.

"They'll come," he told me, "but we'll give them a reception. It's a pity you're leaving right now, when the party is about to start."

5

The Cuban Challenge

From August 2 to August 20, 1961, Guevara went through an experience of intense political and personal involvement. For the rest of his full life he would remember this period as one of the most exciting he had known. It was at this time that President John F. Kennedy launched his ambitious project, Alliance for Progress, at the beach resort of Punta del Este, Uruguay.

Guevara and I had separated only four months before in Havana, but during that time an event of tremendous historical importance had taken place, and I was anxious to see him. In April the United States had finally invaded Cuba, using an expeditionary force made up of exiled Cubans. It was crushed shortly after landing.

This event had heated the tensions of the hemisphere to a danger point. The anti-American feeling of the masses south of Río Bravo was running high, and there was a serious decline in the influence of the United States the world over. The program of the Alliance for Progress was a counter-move to remedy this situation. Like many of President Kennedy's proposals, it seemed to be a product of good intentions, rather than a reflection of the true foreign policy of the United States.

116

Yet no one could doubt that this project, improvised by Kennedy's advisers to fill the immense gap opened by the abortive invasion, would be set in motion. We must remember that Argentina and Brazil, the two largest countries of Latin America, shared the general ideas embodied in the proposal. The presidents of these countries appeared to have invisible ties with the American government. The failure of the invasion had weakened Kennedy's position, and one way for him to regain lost ground was through a lasting alliance with the two major countries of the south. These, in turn, were being governed by highly controversial men, reformists of a new generation who had stumbled into many obstacles in their work. Having Kennedy's support improved their chances of finishing out their presidential terms, which were in serious jeopardy.

This was the picture when Guevara left Havana at midnight on August 2, 1961, in a commercial aircraft of the Cuban Airlines. Days before he had written to his mother telling her he wanted to see the whole family in Punta del Este. He asked her also to let me know he was coming, which she did immediately.

There were certain countries with which Cuba no longer maintained relations, and others whose relations with Cuba were extremely shaky. The Britannia carrying Guevara and forty-four companions, among them economic advisers, officials from the Cuban ministries, journalists, and body-guards, could not expect a friendly welcome on the regular route to Uruguay. So it stopped in Dutch Guiana, a jungle-ridden country with barely a quarter of a million inhabitants, a people divided by color and by several languages and dialects. Even here a nationalist delegation came to Guevara's plane to give him a symbolic carved oar, like those used by the colony's natives in their dugouts.

The Cuban delegation seemed to be the one center of interest at the conference. This was evident along the highway joining Montevideo and Punta del Este, which I drove over only a few hours ahead of Guevara and his entourage. It was lined from one end to the other with a multitude of factory workers and students holding up Cuban flags and pro-Cuban signs. The Government feared the heavy mood of violence and almost immediately ordered the police to block all access to the highway and maintain strict control over vehicles and pedestrians.

I met Guevara in the hall where the sessions were to be held. Though a large auditorium, it was not big enough for the mass of delegates and officials stirring about and talking in front of a platform adorned with the national flags of the hemisphere. We did not have a chance to really talk until that night.

Winter next to the sea is particularly severe in the South Atlantic, and Guevara's chronic asthma had flared up the moment he arrived. That evening he was forced to retire for several hours. I went up to his room on the second floor of the Hotel Playa, a deteriorated villa whose only apparent good point was its isolation. It stood apart from the mass of buildings at the beach resort. The Cuban delegation occupied one whole floor of the hotel, and its members had faithfully reproduced the organizational arrangement of Ché's offices in Havana. It was a cross between an army bivouac and a government bureau, typists mixed with machine gun-toting guards. Some prepared meals, others handled the telephones, and all of them moved with a timing hardly to be expected among so many people squeezed into such a tight space.

Guevara was in bed that night, but his usual good humor tried to break through the painful attacks of asthma. He told me that on a visit to Peking his asthma had struck while he was in conference with Mao Tse-tung. The fit was so violent that he left as if his heart would stop and he would collapse before the Chinese head of state. This incident had really alarmed Mao. He insisted Guevara could be cured with acupuncture, the universal remedy of the Chinese, a treatment in which the nervous system is stimulated with pins. But Guevara's ailment had defeated Mao's doctors.

"Do you see?" Guevara remarked, his face tightened into a pained smile. "This damn asthma has resisted even the Chinese, and they're just about impossible to resist."

In spite of his physical condition, a superhuman load of work awaited him at Punta del Este. All the intrigues, passions, rancors, and hopes of Latin American politics had been poured into the crucible of the Building of the Americas, where the assembly met, and in two dozen private residences where secret huddles and conspiracies took place at any time of day.

Shortly after arriving, I had been stopped in a corridor by an old acquaintance, Jorge Carretoni, a member of President Frondizi's radical party who, after many years as a deputy, represented the government in special negotiations. He asked me to introduce him to Guevara, begging me to do it outside the assembly building, since he wanted to talk in private.

When I told Guevara about this, he said he wanted to know the point of the interview beforehand. There were always quite a few Argentines stumbling over each other in the ante-rooms trying to shake Ché's hand. That night I explained to Carretoni that he ought to supply more information, and he answered:

"I'm on a confidential mission for Frondizi."

The interview took place the following day in Guevara's room: Guevara, Carretoni, and myself. For a long while it remained a cordial conversation among friends, *mate* in hand and a pot of hot water ready for refills. Then I offered to leave so that they could speak alone, a suggestion rejected by both men. Thus I was present at the first indirect contact between Frondizi and Guevara, which would lead to a real meeting between them a few days later in Buenos Aires.

President Frondizi's invitation did not have official status, and there were two conditions attached: Guevara should receive an official invitation from Brazil before going to Buenos Aires, and his trip to Argentina should be made as discreetly as possible, both in entering and in leaving the country.

From the head of the Brazilian delegation, the Minister of Economy, Clementi Mariani, Guevara had already received a verbal invitation to visit President Quadros in Brazilia, and this was officially confirmed the following day. Guevara was not in a position to dictate his own terms for a meeting with Frondizi. He asked to be taken from Punta del Este straight to Buenos Aires, and from there back to Montevideo, since he did not want to miss the chance to use his interview with Frondizi to promote relations between Cuba and Uruguay. He also wanted to travel accompanied by the Director of Latin American Affairs for the Cuban government, the efficient Ramón Aja Castro.

From the moment the interview with Frondizi was arranged, the few of us who knew about it and about his future visit to Quadros watched several sub-plots unfolding, each occurring simultaneously with the main story. This, in the world's eyes, was still the Alliance for Progress.

Guevara made a detailed analysis of the American project after it had been presented by the head of the United States delegation, Douglas Dillon. He compared Cuba's progress in two years of revolution with the progress promised to Latin America; he was skeptical about whether the aid funds mentioned would ever be delivered; and he outlined the basis on which Cuba would once more consider its participation in inter-American plans. (The impact of his address was indicated a few hours after the session, when the most powerful economist at this time, Raúl Prebisch, Secretary General of the Economic Commission to the United Nations for Latin America, asked me to arrange a personal meeting for him with Guevara.)

Without losing a certain Cuban cadence he had acquired, Guevara gave a very concise speech, outstanding in its economy of adjectives and its restrained tone. One could read between the lines that Cuba had settled down to wait for Guevara's interviews with Presidents Frondizi and Quadros, and that, essentially, the idea of a Pan-American system reconstructed under the Kennedy spirit wasn't entirely objectionable to Havana. On condition, of course, that Cuba's socialist form of government be respected.

Lest his sober oratory be interpreted as an unusual show of Cuba's weakness, Guevara ended by dealing the American delegates a blow. He read a secret document on the economic development of Venezuela. This paper had been drawn up by two American officials, and it concluded on a strong note of pessimism about the success of the measures adopted by Venezuela. When Guevara read it, the American delegates turned pale. Robert Woodward, Assistant Secretary of State for Latin American Affairs, later said that there was no such document and that Guevara had read the resume of an article published by *The New York Times*. Dillon himself stated that if it was actually a legitimate official American document, it was nothing but the opinion of a minor official. The discomfiture of the American delegation lasted until the end of the conference, when it was established that the report was indeed authentic, and that it had been sent to Ambassador Teodoro Moscoso and stolen from his car just before the Venezuelan students burned the car at the gates of the University campus in Caracas. A month later the controversy loosed in Venezuela by this incident was still going strong and causing disturbances. But compared with those that occurred in Argentina and Brazil, these seemed insignificant.

While Frondizi's emissary was on his way to Buenos Aires to confirm the details of the interview with Guevara, news was received of a military uprising in Argentina. Around midnight on August 11th, just after part of the Cuban delegation had sat down to dinner, someone reported that the government radio stations in Buenos Aires were broadcasting military marches and the text of a rebel proclamation. I was eating with Guevara that night, and after exchanging glances we dashed out of the room. The news dropped like a bomb among the large concentration of diplomats and economists at Punta del Este. Few of them got any sleep that night until the radio stations returned to government control at dawn, and it was announced that the *putsch* had failed completely.

Guevara's visit to Buenos Aires presented many problems, among them small details like the question of the document of identity he would use to enter the country. He had a Cuban diplomat passport, but this would have to be visaed at the Argentine Embassy in Montevideo, and in that event the strict secrecy Frondizi had stamped on the whole arrangement would be compromised. Carretoni, the trouble-laden lawyer, decided to take Ché's passport to Montevideo and ask the Argentine ambassador to put his visa on the document. The ambassador, an elderly man who belonged to the old guard of the radical party, was stunned when he saw who the traveler was. He asked for time to think it over and immediately sent a coded cable to the Argentine chancellor, asking for his authorization to issue the visa "to the head of the Cuban delegation." The request took the lid off the secret, since code service at the Ministry is in the hands of army officers attached to the intelligence service. From this moment on the Argentine secret service and, of course, the CIA knew that Guevara would be going to Buenos Aires. If the scandal did not break then, it was because the military brass felt they could use it better against Frondizi later, and they let the meeting take place.

While the discussions of the statesmen labored on, the work of the delegations at Punta del Este fell off noticeably. Social life took up more and more of the delegates' time; there was a constant round of barbecues à la créole and parties at night.

The President of Uruguay, an entertaining politician who had been a nationalist at one time, organized a reception in his magnificent beach house. Guevara was amused by Eduardo Haedo's character and personality, because they reminded him of the old Argentine politicians he had known as a boy, in the province of Córdoba. They were soon on intimate terms, egging each other on in tests of wits.

Guevara explained that they planned to make Cuba a big producer of nickel when the first five-year plan ended.

"Are the deposits in the south?" Haedo asked.

"Well, Cuba doesn't have a south," Guevara answered, tracing an imaginary sketch of the island.

"But it does have a north," the Uruguayan President added maliciously.

"And it also has an *Oriente* . . ." Ché emphasized with equal irony.

On his return to Havana Guevara mentioned on television his meeting with Haedo and recalled him as someone who "likes a good wisecrack, with whom we had a good time exchanging quips and drinking *mate*."

He was less amused by the Uruguayan chancellor. The latter had been somewhat aggressive in his response to Guevara's statistics of the Cuban population.

"Are you counting those who left?"

"No," Guevara replied serenely, "No, not those. We only count the ones who come back."

Everyone understood that Guevara was referring to the hundreds of prisoners who had capitulated a few months before, when the invasion fell through.

More discreet, and less cutting, was Guevara's conversation with President Kennedy's special assistant on Latin American affairs, Richard N. Goodwin. In spite of the efforts made later, both in Cuba and in the United States, to minimize the importance of that meeting, the fact remains that Goodwin was the person who represented Kennedy in the plenary sessions of the *Consejo Revolucionario Cubano* (Cuban Revolutionary Council), the exile committee, and had been the organizer of the abortive invasion. He could be considered Kennedy's number-one expert on Cuban affairs; whatever the diplomatic informality and language difficulties of his conversation with Guevara, it had to take on extraordinary meaning. One thing it did was confirm Guevara's hypothesis that his interviews with Frondizi and Quadros had Kennedy's blessing.

The game was organized so that all the participants supported one another. Quadros' invitation and the conversation with Goodwin protected Frondizi. The audience with Frondizi and the meeting with Goodwin covered Quadros. And should the United States Senate want to know the reasons behind Goodwin's contact with Ché, Kennedy could fall back on the fact that Guevara had been received by the presidents of Argentina and Brazil.

The thing was, this whole delicate apparatus of counterbalances had to be put in motion at the right speed; otherwise, it could fall apart at any moment, at grave risk to each of the protagonists, Guevara excepted, of course.

On August 18, 1961, Guevara was flown to Buenos Aires in a small plane chartered by the Argentine government. With him were Aja Castro, the Cuban, and the Argentine negotiator, Carretoni.

In Buenos Aires a small escort was waiting under the command of President Frondizi's military aide, an army colonel. This man had been entrusted with the special mission of picking up an important arrival at the small Don Torquato Airport, some twenty miles from the capital—no mention of his name. To his immense surprise, the colonel saw through the airplane's open door a man in a green uniform, bearded, wearing an open topcoat and a beret with a gleaming major's star. His amazement grew when he recognized Ché. Suddenly dumbstruck, he doffed his own military cap twice, extending his gloved hand in an involuntary movement. Guevara immediately understood the colonel's plight and put out his own hand in a matter-of-fact way.

"I'm Major Guevara, Colonel. That's your car, isn't it?"

President Frondizi was impatiently awaiting Ché's arrival in his official residence, Olivos, a small country estate a few minutes from downtown Buenos Aires. As long as Guevara was on Argentine soil, Frondizi had to consider the possibility of an attempt on the Cuban's life, plotted by the military intelligence service. But he didn't tell anyone about this fear, not even his closest colleagues or members of his family.

Guevara and Frondizi spoke behind closed doors for an hour and twenty minutes. The old but ever-present theme of Latin American development was the first thing they discussed.

"Argentina has chosen the road of gradual independence," Frondizi said. "At the moment, we plan to stop the importation of oil. It costs us two hundred million dollars a year."

"Cuba is in the same spot," Guevara answered, "but from previous experience we know better than to insist on investing American capital. Perhaps you'd be interested in knowing about our experience, since Cuba had one of the highest investments of American capital. The amounts of capital invested were always less than those recorded in the books. Consequently, the profits were transferred on the basis of an overstated capital. Utilizing internal credit, American interests enjoyed a monopolistic position in the market and took away more than they brought in."

Both men were passionately interested in economics, but the interview was to have a different subject. Frondizi made his point very clear.

"It would be unacceptable to the Americas," he said, "if Cuba or any other of our countries joined an extracontinental military organization. There's fear in the air that Cuba will decide to join the Warsaw Pact. If it takes this step, its return to the inter-American family will become impossible."

"That's an assumption we haven't encouraged," Guevara answered. "It was invented by the actual aggressors of our country.

It's a fact that Cuba has military assistance from the Soviet Union and the other socialist countries. As for a strict military association, sealed by a treaty, they're not asking for it, and Cuba is not offering it. No doubt it's inconceivable to the United States that one country can help another militarily without binding it in every respect."

The Argentine President also asked about the possibility of a gradual reconstruction in Cuba of a representative democratic system, with electoral bodies and parliamentary chambers. Guevara said that that road could never be followed again because now political representation in Cuba was founded on other principles.

"In Cuba we're afraid that any vacillation on this point would sink the country into the old destructive disputes between parties and factions. Cuba was plagued by parties and pressure groups that neutralized the best efforts of its people. Those of us in power have been fighting for two years to erase this image of politics. And on no account will we give way on this point!"

While the two men avidly discussed Latin American affairs, the present and the future of Argentina and Cuba, a storm of excitement was beginning to whirl through the offices of the ministers and military staff, the information agencies and the embassies.

"Ché is here!"

When they left the meeting room, President Frondizi's wife and daughter greeted Guevara amiably. It was midday.

"Wouldn't you like to have a good steak right now?" the President's wife asked.

"Wouldn't I!" Guevara exclaimed. And, recalling the Argentine custom of serving grilled meat with potatoes and fried eggs, he added, "A good steak *a caballo*, a fine idea."

It was the last meal Ché would have in Buenos Aires.

He requested one more favor of Frondizi: he wanted to visit

a sick aunt, who would probably die soon. Although their agreement stipulated that Guevara leave the capital immediately, Frondizi granted this request, and Ché rode in a car through the streets of the city he had left eight years before.

In the meantime the excitement was growing.

"Ché is here!"

At noon, the Argentinian Chancellor, Adolfo Mugica, admitted that Guevara had had an interview with the President. He was as confused as the rest of the country, and he resigned hours later, not as a sign of disapproval, but as a means of saving face, since he had been one of the last to learn about the meeting.

But Guevara was already flying back to Montevideo. From there, not wasting any time, he left for Brazilia.

There an act shorter than the one in Buenos Aires took place, though in the end it was much more dramatic. On August 19th in an improvised ceremony in Brazilia's Planelto Palace, President Janio Quadros granted Guevara the *Orden Nacional do Cruzeiro do Sul*. (Quadros had just formulated an appeal to the Soviet Union for aid in Brazil's development, alleging that Western cooperation was insufficient.) Not only had Guevara been unaware that he would receive a decoration, he did not even know the nature of the meeting. He was unprepared to decorate the President in return, as is customary, and Quadros' speech was extremely brief. Ché decided to answer with the same brevity, accepting the distinction as having been given to the revolutionary government and the Cuban people, thus depriving it of any personal importance.

Guevara's conversation with Quadros centered on the same subjects discussed with Frondizi: the advisability of not joining the Warsaw Pact, insinuations about representative democracy, an open door for Cuba in the inter-American organization.

In Rio de Janeiro and Sao Paulo, crowds poured into the streets. They carried big photographs of Ché as well as Cuban flags.

The scandal was as great as the one in Argentina, and a week after Guevara's visit, under threats from the Right, Quadros resigned in an inexplicable fit of bitterness.

In Washington, the third and invisible associate involved in Ché's tour, John F. Kennedy, also had to face personal attacks. The Cuban exiles, angry at Kennedy's refusal to bomb their own country, led the agitation. And in the United States Senate, conspiracies were hatched to back the President against the wall.

One president, Quadros, had been unable to hold his ground after Ché's visit and resigned a week later. Another, Frondizi, was heavily attacked for the same reason and overthrown in less than seven months. A third, Kennedy, whose lot it was to play the double role of armed invader and diplomatic intermediary, was assassinated two years afterwards, in a dark plot in which relations with Cuba played a very important part.

"As for me, I won't die in bed," Ché said to me. This was said in Montevideo after some thugs had fired on the participants at a mass rally Ché was attending at the university, near the end of the Punta del Este conference. It was never established whether or not the attackers were trying to kill Ché. They murdered a professor and wounded some other people.

But by that time Guevara already had so many battle scars on his body that when the shots rang out around him, he did not lose his self-possession. From the *Granma* landing he had kept two souvenirs: a bullet that hit the cartilage of his left ear, down by the neck, penetrating his body to come out through his shoulder blade, and another that hit him in the chest, no doubt with very little force.

Referring to this wound, he once told me, "I read somewhere that the bullet was stopped by a religious medal I was wearing around my neck. I've never worn any kind of medal. Actually, the bullet rammed itself into an Argentine identity card I carried in my shirt pocket. It was the card the police in the province of

Cordoba had issued to me when I was in high school. It was made up of two thick pieces of pressed cardboard. I was really saved that day, pal, because I was an Argentine."

He also had a bullet wound in one foot. He got that one in a battle near the Sierra Maestra in December 1957.

And finally, there was the wound he received accidentally during the Bay of Pigs invasion.

"I was in a cabin, near the coast, waiting for those bastards to come along. Suddenly, a shot. I tasted blood running down my face. I yelled: Get him! thinking it was an attack. But no, it was my own pistol. It had dropped to the floor cocked, along with the double belt I've always worn loosely. It went off when it struck the ground. The bullet hit my cheek, but if it had strayed one centimeter, it would have torn into the base of my brain."

This man, toughened by war, had been assigned one of the most delicate and exacting diplomatic missions of recent times. Between them, violence and his own intelligence were the counterpoint of Ernesto Guevara's life.

6

A Program for Revolution

1963 turned out to be a year of great turbulence throughout Latin America. In the Valle de la Convencion, in the ancient Cuzco of the Incas, peasants were fighting under the leadership of a man who had organized the first agrarian unions in Peru. An agriculture student who had attended the university in Argentina, Hugo Blanco was making the most of a set of conditions similar to those in Cuba during the Castro revolution: a military government rejected by the middle class, students fighting the regime in the streets, and peasant masses looking for organization and political leadership.

In Brazil the organization of peasant leagues was growing with the quasi-approval of President Joao Goulart, a nationalist who depended more and more on the leftists among the unions and the intellectuals.

In Venezuela the apparatus of the powerful Communist Party had thrown itself headlong into the fight against President Romulo Betancourt's government. It had the cooperation of malcontents of every stripe, all apparently ready to unite into a single ideological and military force.

130

Argentina too appeared to be on the verge of civil war. The overthrown President Frondizi was a prisoner of the armed forces, on the lonely island of Martín García on the River Plate. Hundreds of factories had shut down because of the shortage of work, thousands of industries were only partially functioning, and no fewer than six hundred thousand unemployed roamed the cities and towns looking for work. Something entirely unprecedented was taking place in the armed forces. Committees of sergeants were formed in the air force, and cells of sailors were formed in the navy. One of the many plots organized by the air force commanders was crushed by a group of non-coms who arrested their officers at pistol point. And on navy ships, printed sheets were circulated in which a mutiny was urged, should the fleet be directed to the Caribbean, where the crisis of October 1962 had opened the way for a possible multilateral armed intervention against Cuba. Finally, daily crowds of unemployed workers throughout the country started to demand arms. In short, no less than four military conspiracies were in the making, and the new government could not settle down to a steady course.

It was during this time that I received a message: Guevara had to see me right away. The messenger handed me an airplane ticket to Havana and told me I was to leave as soon as possible. I did.

The ostracism of Cuba at this time became abundantly clear to anyone who tried to go to Havana from any other Latin American country. My itinerary took in Prague, Czechoslavakia, by way of Shannon, Ireland, and Oxford, Canada. But the difficulties imposed by the American blockade against the island could be seen even better when the Cuban airplane ran into mechanical trouble and needed repairs and new parts. Our aircraft's de-icing system had broken down as the plane flew below the Arctic Circle, and it was forced to land at Gander, Newfoundland. There was a huge American base there on skeleton staff. During

World War II it had served as a hopping point for the Flying Fortresses that bombed the European continent. The storerooms were packed with spare parts, but the authorities refused to supply any, and the Cuban airplane had to remain a week in this bleak part of Newfoundland, twenty-five degrees below zero, until a Canadian plane came back with the necessary part.

The extent of the blockade became fully apparent at the airport in Havana; the war fever it had aroused was obvious. An immense poster proclaimed: "Country or Death." On another could be read: "To Arms." When I arrived, a little more than two months had gone by since the dramatic missile crisis, when Kennedy and Khrushchev had discussed Cuba's fate, and the whole world had swayed for several days on the edge of nuclear war; although the tension was much lower now, it wasn't difficult to imagine how high it had soared in October.

The government official whom Guevara had sent to meet me said I'd be staying in the district of Cubanacán, the new name for what had been the elegant suburb where the island's rich had built their huge mansions. Although I did not understand the meaning of this invitation right away, Guevara himself explained it to me a few hours later.

"You've been kidnapped, Fatso," he laughed. "You're at my mercy, but don't get scared. I had you come here only so we could talk."

And that's how it turned out: long, involved conversations about Latin America in general and Argentina in particular. They went on from February 2nd to April 10, 1963. Guevara and I examined the problems of Latin revolution, the present and the future of Cuba, and his own situation.

Guevara was certain that the capitalist world would never again submit tamely to the tutelage of the United States, and he felt that Cuba ought to take advantage of this fact. As an example, he pointed out that President Kennedy was being urged by many to take reprisals against France for its support of Cuba, but Guevara believed this couldn't be done. Any sanctions of the USSR against China seemed equally impossible. There was a difference in the two situations, of course. The conflict between the socialist nations concerned something more important for Guevara: the power of the international proletariat. And so, in the splitting up of alliances after the war, Cuba found, on the one hand, new opportunities to assert its independence, but on the other, new reasons to fear isolation. Being part of a discordant family, with many quarrels impossible to cover up, in which the divisive faults of the capitalist countries were apparent, was a situation that sank Guevara in deep gloom.

It led him to one conclusion: Cuba needed to repair its ties with Latin America, but only after social revolutions had come to the other countries, for these ties could no longer be based on relations between countries with different political concepts.

Guevara had been carefully examining the real conditions in Latin America, trying to find out what could be done along such lines. Since capitalist Latin America rejected coexistence with socialist Cuba, Cuba would help all revolutionaries wipe out capitalism in their countries.

My first long discussion with Guevara centered on the missile crisis. Russia had offered the missiles in order to preserve Cuba's military security, and they had arrived on the island at the beginning of October 1962. The launching pads were built in a wooded zone near the city of San Cristobal and were soon in condition to fire middle range missiles on Washington. But on October 28th, faced by a threatening note from the United States, Khrushchev agreed to withdraw them, and within seventy-two hours the forty-two Russian missiles were inside the holds of the same ships that had brought them.

"When Fidel got the news," Ché told me, "he wouldn't believe it. He learned it from a foreign newspaperman asking on the telephone for confirmation. The journalists had received advance notice of the official Soviet announcement that the missiles were being withdrawn, and a few minutes later he read Fidel the complete text of the cable. There could be no doubt. The Russians had decided a Cuban problem without consulting us. Fidel swore, as I did, and to get rid of the tension he whirled around quickly and kicked the wall. A huge mirror hung in that spot. It was shattered by the impact and crashed in a noisy shower of glass. We remained silent a moment and, calmed down, began to study the situation."

My own explanation of the Soviet move, I told Guevara, was very similar to the Russians', although I was not trying to side with them. The way I saw it, the problem of the missiles had been artificially created by the Russians in order to distract attention from their discussion with Kennedy about the future of Cuba. If they had not created the missile crisis, the discussion would have had to get down to the real question, that is, the very survival of Castro's regime. This way, the Russians gave Kennedy a diplomatic victory without that victory also meaning the end of Cuban socialism.

"Could be," Guevara murmured, "but that's not the real question. The real question is, Must Cuba give up its sovereignty to the Russians? Is it possible they don't understand that this country has had too many kinds of paternalism from the great powers to accept a new one silently? How can I explain it to you? This is basically a philosophical question. If there is no understanding of national peculiarities within international socialism, we might as well give up; the socialist nations will feel that they are being treated as small countries by big powers to whom being big is more important than being socialist."

Guevara was still confident that the Russians would not barter Cuba for any other situation in the rest of the world, just as he

had assured me two years previously. But he was afraid that
Soviet protection might stand in the way of Cuba's development
as an autonomous nation. It is in this light that one can explain
two incidents that occurred later that year: first, the Cubans' refusal to subscribe to the anti-atomic pact promoted by the Russians, and second, the anger of their discussions about the terms
of Soviet aid to repair the damages caused by a hurricane.

The struggle to maintain a national identity was also evident
in more basic forms. Cigarettes, for example. The old brands,
generally American, had been replaced by others unmistakably
Cuban: Armoas, Dorados, and Criollos. Gangster and cowboy
films remained in the files of television stations, and the previous
torrent of commercial publicity that had made the neon signs of
Havana a match for those of New York or Miami had virtually
disappeared. The prolonged reign of English as the universal
language of business and consumer economy was no more: the
new advertising and, in general, the names of the stores were
in Spanish.

It was, in a way, a blockade from within, the Cuban answer
to the blockade from without that reached its high point in 1963,
although it was never total. Cars covered with dents, half painted,
with soldered seams and patchwork, passed through the streets of
Havana. The doors of mass-transportation vehicles closed badly
and noisily, their motors barely held up under the constant usage
and the shortage of spare parts. In the fields hundreds of tractors
stood immobilized, serving as lonely workshops for mechanics
removing parts needed for other vehicles.

There was no one reason for this situation, it was a combination
of factors. The blockade was the main one, along with the fear
it produced among many of the best technicians, who began
looking for a way to emigrate and generally found it. But another
important factor was the crisis of production and organization

brought on by the inexperience of the administrators appointed by the revolution.

"To start Cuba's industries rolling," Guevara reflected, "we have to produce construction materials: cement, bricks, tiles. Right now we have two big kilns standing still because we haven't been able to get the fire-bricks. We even have to improvise screws. Some textile plants have closed because of the uneven quality of the thread. And in the shoe industry we're trying to extricate ourselves from the mess we got into when an official ordered the closing of the small workshops before the big ones had started to operate."

As Minister of Industries Guevara used all his imagination and energy to solve the multitude of problems that snarled up Cuba's industrial economy. He was unsparing in his demands, but everyone accepted them without protest because they always began with himself. And yet, were I to draw a conclusion about Guevara's state of mind during those months—when we saw each other every day—I would say that the struggle was undermining his optimism. His ingenuity seemed blunted, his spirit smothered under the mountains of statistics and production methods. Before the missile crisis the thought that Cuba might still expect an armed attack from the United States had maintained a solid bond between Guevara the fighter and Guevara the Minister of Industry. But in 1963 he began to notice that the stability of the Cuban regime depended, to a great extent, on the worldwide interplay of forces, in which Cuba could not change a thing without risk of national suicide.

There were others who also noticed Cuba's new situation, among them the defeated and revengeful Cuban exiles, a group whose internal schisms made them a real exception among exiled communities of this century. After 1917 the Russian nobility had adapted itself to life in the great European cities. At the other social extreme the Spanish Republicans had contributed their labor to the industrial establishments of Europe and the Americas. Among the middle class or among the workers they all found a place. But the mixed contingent of Cubans in the United States seemed destined only to serve the interests of some American politicians, who instigated them against what was already beginning to be called "the appeasement of Castro."

Guevara informed me one night that a break was fast coming between Kennedy and the coordinating council of Cuban exiles, a body with undefined notions in which no fewer than two hundred anti-Castro organizations were represented, all of them equally vague, many of them organizations in name only.

"The funniest thing about all this is that Miró Cardona, who gathers all those worms together," laughed Guevara, his cigar between his lips, "is the same person who signed the decree granting me Cuban citizenship. Can you beat that? And the other, well, the other was Urrutia. Imagine."

The pressure from Kennedy's enemies gave the Cuban exiles the leverage they needed to make things difficult for the President. One day in February we listened to a direct transmission of one of Kennedy's speeches, in which he tried to calm down those of his countrymen who believed, or pretended to believe, that there would be an armed attack from Cuba. The man in the street had been led by the press to fear for his life each night he went to bed, because little Cuba had a hundred MIG fighters, five hundred air-to-earth missiles, and fifteen hundred rockets for coastal defense. These modest figures grew inordinately in the minds of the Americans who temporarily forgot the colossal military machine of their own country. It was to them Kennedy addressed himself when he said there was nothing to be afraid of, that five thousand Russian soldiers had left the island and a few thousand more were simply training Cuban soldiers, without themselves forming combat units.

This was one of the paradoxes to be experienced in Cuba: the tiny country making the powerful neighbor lose its composure.

It was more understandable that our old friend Betancourt should lose his composure.

"Look!" Guevara handed me a cable, a gleam in his eyes. "Look at what the Venezuelan revolutionaries have just done. Rómulo will be sick today."

The news was spectacular. A handful of men had captured a five-thousand-ton ship under full steam on its way to Houston. They were sailing it toward an unknown destination, with the entire world following its track. Betancourt had recently announced his trip to the United States for a conference with Kennedy, and this incident would undoubtedly damage his prestige. Hundreds of bombs were exploding in Caracas.

Guevara still harbored a dislike for Betancourt, dating back to the days when we knew him in Costa Rica.

"I distrusted him then, remember? Not now. Now I'm *sure* he's our worst enemy, the enemy of all anti-imperialist revolutions of Latin America. And it's a very personal thing, believe me. His arrogance blinds him, it keeps him from seeing clearly when his own person is at stake. He's not lying when he maintains that he's defending the individual against socialism. But the individual he's defending is himself. An individualist no matter what the consequences, right?"

Another of our friends from the past was elected President of the Dominican Republic that year. In March, Juan Bosch, the mulatto who used to discuss literature with Guevara, began an arduous government, which he eventually had to leave unfinished.

It was then Ché asked me to discuss Argentina's problems with him, systematically. He felt a greater interest in the country of his birth than he had shown up to then. Why? I did not know, unless it was the obvious fact that internal chaos was continuing to rise in Argentina. But Guevara wanted to examine the matter as clearly as possible, in all its details. During this period of discussion, he used to take notes from time to time. The labor and university movements were his principal interest. He also wanted to know about those engaged in politics. Many, if not most of them, had not been in politics when he left Argentina. And others, whose names he remembered, were only that, names to remember, forgotten personalities

Guevara refused to admit that one exceptional condition on which Castro's revolutionaries had relied was the nature of the Cuban army. It had been very well armed, of course, and very numerous. But its similarities to other armies, the Argentine, to begin with, stopped there. You could not seriously talk about the feeling of unity of the Cuban military, because favoritism was so rife. You could not say it had a historical tradition, because the Cuban army had been organized no less than three times in the short history of the island, and all three times set up by the military themselves. And although the Argentine army had produced some of the country's biggest reactionaries, it was also true that President Juan Peron, the idol of the masses, boasted the rank of General. Peron was still a formidable threat in the event of a fight against the army.

"Suppose Peron were to leave his exile in Spain," Guevara said, "and settle here in Havana. Do you think this would change the attitude of the Argentine masses?"

I did not believe so, and I explained why. First, I didn't think it was really possible that Peron would leave Spain for Cuba, even if the admiration Peron professed for Castro and the Cuban revolutionaries, expressed in a letter Ché had in his possession, were sincere. Second, I didn't think the Argentine army was in such a state of decay that it would surrender before using all the political means at its disposal.

On April 2, 1963, in the middle of our discussions, the Argentine navy, together with a group of high ranking officers in the army and air force, tried to take over the government in Buenos

Aires. There was a battle, and the navy's planes bombed the army garrisons. Columns of tanks immediately attacked the navy bases and destroyed them. Civil war hovered over Argentina. At the gates of the garrisons the soldiers' mothers held noisy demonstrations against fratricidal war, and a tacit feeling of protest filtered through all sectors of society.

Guevara was convinced that the situation in Argentina was growing ripe for popular revolution.

"The objective conditions for the struggle are beginning to appear in Argentina," Ché speculated. "There's unemployment and therefore hunger, and the working class is starting to react to this. Such reaction sets off repressive measures, and repression stirs up hatred. That's the exact point at which objective conditions need reinforcement with subjective ones, that is, with an awareness of the possibility of victory by violent means, in the face of imperialists and their allies within the country."

It was one of the central themes of Guevara's revolutionary thought and the crux of every controversy that has rocked Latin America in the last few years: Can a nucleus of armed rebels use subjective means to bring to a head the objective revolutionary conditions that exist to some extent in all Latin countries?

The case of Argentina gave the question an added interest, not only because Guevara and I knew it well, but also because, from my point of view, Argentina combined a set of conditions that could make it something more than an exception to Guevara's theory, if not the antithesis of the Cuban model.

Guevara rejected the idea of an exception whenever we discussed it. He always rejected it, for Cuba as well as any other country. More than anything else it seemed a refusal to recognize anything that might be taken as a justification for the revolutionary inactivity of the Left in Latin America. In the end Guevara had to admit that, in Cuba's case, the United States had been caught off-guard, looking the other way, and no one could now imagine that the Americans would again be caught in the same manner.

Since the principal economic sector in Argentina was the countryside, Guevara reasoned that the armed struggle should be based there. He imagined a peasant army taking over the cities. He refused to admit that the structure of agrarian property over a good part of Argentine land is formed by small and moderately prosperous landowners, and by tenant farmers who benefit from low rents. This majority has shaped the topography of the most important regions of the country with its wealth as well as the density of its population. The latter was another factor that Guevara underestimated, possibly because he involuntarily applied the conditions of rural Cuba to the rest of Latin America. In Argentina the areas where a large concentration of the proletariat is engaged in agriculture are the cotton fields and the grain country, the sugar plantations and the hard timber forests. The size of the country itself converts these centers into tiny islands, easy to surround and crush should a movement based on the nucleus theory try to get a foothold in any of them. Only a large organization with national influence could simultaneously set in motion the various sectors in which there is potential revolutionary energy.

As a rule, the agrarian population of Argentina reproduces the social characteristics of the urban population. The predominant part of the population belongs to a middle class, small-propertied or else not propertied but equally well off thanks to partial adjustments in the laws of civil trade or the country's participation in world commerce. These are masses with serious problems of their own, but there is no question that they will let themselves be mobilized only by representative middlemen.

I decided that Guevara could not accept the necessity of a national revolutionary organization for Argentina, because were he to do so, the next step would be a compromise about the formation of political parties as a prerequisite to the armed struggle. And even if he managed in some way of his own to see the impossibility of building a party that represented an alliance of classes with nationalist and anti-imperialist objectives, he would be drawn to a conclusion distasteful to him: the revolutionary party would run the danger of being absorbed by the Communist Party, and Guevara had little faith in the revolutionary capacity of the latter.

There was still another conclusion that surely haunted Ché, although he could hardly bring himself to formulate, much less discuss it. It was that Cuba had abused the exceptional conditions which had made the revolution possible, and, accordingly, it could not serve as an example for other Latin American countries. For the United States, on the other hand, it had indeed served as an example.

"That's true," Guevara admitted. "Imperialism has learned a lot more from the Cuban experience than have the revolutionaries on our own continent."

A sample of this capacity to learn was shown at the beginning of April 1963, when Kennedy's government announced that it had adopted certain measures to suppress the exile pirate raids into Cuban territory. It was clearly one way of confirming the existence of a nonaggression pact against Cuba. Washington now trusted the passage of time.

". . . and time works in favor of socialism," added Guevara, for whom time was a dynamic concept, in no way static. "The Russians propose that we let time pass, our arms crossed, and we insist on prodding time, urging the revolution on. . . ."

Time had also passed for me, and I was being called back to Buenos Aires. I told Guevara I had to return. First, however, he wanted me to attend a cannon and mortar target practice that was to be held along the coast near Havana.

We went there the next morning at dawn. There were a hundred men engaging in rapid-fire exercise. After a while a mortar jammed. Volunteers were needed to extract the shell from the firing tube. Many hands went up, each man showing himself ready to run the risk of death entailed in defusing a mortar. It was an unforgettable scene. Wasn't this the model of the New Man Guevara wanted to build in Cuba and, through socialism, in all of Latin America? A brave and responsible man, a good worker with an open character, with dignity and a sense of humor, unselfish, intelligent, ready for any sacrifice. Was this Utopian, the dialectical answer to the other Latin American man Guevara had seen: undernourished, afraid of the powerful, his intelligence clouded by ignorance and hunger?

Guevara embodied a good portion of these virtues of the man of the future. He forced himself to extremes that seemed inexplicable, or at least not very practical.

The day before I left Cuba, I was with Guevara when his wife called him on the phone to ask him for his official car so she could go shopping in the city.

"No, Aleida," Ché answered. "You know the car belongs to the government, not to me. You can't use it. Take the bus like everyone else."

Later on this domestic incident led to a family discussion during which both Aleida and Ché's mother, Celia, revealed that he was very careful not to use his position in the government to obtain more than he needed to live on. His house, a mansion confiscated from a rich exile, was practically bare, despite the innumerable gifts he was always receiving on his international tours. These gifts, ranging from decorative items to handicrafts and electrical appliances, Ché sent to the training centers for young people throughout the island. They ended up there exactly as he had received them, without even being opened. Seeing the ascetic rooms of his house, I couldn't forget the room in La Paz where I had met him, where a single nail in the wall was the extent of the furniture.

As an exception, Guevara had kept and wore now a handsome wristwatch, one of fifteen identical wristwatches he had received. He had distributed the others among his best friends, and with the passing of time that watch became a secret badge, a silent means of identity between those who wore it. I was to see others like it later on, in other parts of the world.

On a cool morning Ché came by in his car to take me to the airport. Celia, who had been visiting with her son and her grandchildren, would be traveling with me.

When we got to the airport Guevara shuddered as if a chill had gone through him. I was wearing an Argentine poncho, the kind women weave on rustic looms up in the mountains. I took it off and handed it to him.

"Take this," I told him. "It's from Argentina. It was given to me during a political tour, some time ago. You can have it, that way you'll always own a piece of our country."

"It'll help a lot," Guevara said happily. "The nights are cold in the hills, even in hot countries. The fog sticks to the slopes and gets into your bones."

There were hugs, last minute requests, goodbyes. Before I went up the airplane steps, Guevara said to me:

"You'll see, Argentina's ruling class will never learn anything. Only a revolutionary war will change things."

This was the last sentence I heard from his lips. I might have forgotten it, had I not been thrown in prison on my return to Buenos Aires. Argentina's military thought I was coming back to organize a guerrilla movement, when in reality I was returning from arguing for two months with Guevara about the untimeliness of just such an action.

They had not learned a thing. Guevara was right.

part three

FOMENTING REVOLUTIONS

7

Guerrillas in Argentina

In 1958, when Castro's guerrillas were fighting in the Cuban countryside, an Argentine journalist made the first attempt to establish a new bond between Argentina and Guevara. His objective was to fix the limits of revolutionary action on the continent, to settle whether it was legitimate for a Latin American revolutionary to fight in any country where struggle was apparent. The cultural and political fragmentation Latin America had been forced into over the last century had created doubt in various countries about a revolutionary's right to participate in outside conflicts. As a result of this confusion, when Argentines learned that their fellow countryman Guevara was fighting in Cuba, their first reaction was negative. They were only showing the century-old bias against the formation of a single Latin American nation. And yet, such a concept was one of the fundamental ideas of Simón Bolívar, the Liberator.

The journalist's name was Jorge Masetti, and because of the important part he was to play in Ché's life, and indirectly in his death, the two men can be thought of as inseparately linked, operating in parallel situations.

147

I met Masetti one night in 1957, when Argentina wasn't yet sure if it was heading for civil war. I was still anti-Peron, and Masetti knew it. A former member of the Nationalist Alliance, a Peronista shock troop which the army had besieged and forced to surrender two years before, he could regard me as an enemy.

In August 1957, at Frondizi's orders, I had set up the first solid contact between our Radical Party and the exiled General Peron. This contact would yield a return later on when Frondizi himself was elected president, with the help of a million Peronista votes; for the moment it brought me Masetti.

In those days the La Paz café served as a rendezvous for newsmen, writers and theater people. It was located on Corrientes Street, an avenue very much like Broadway.

It took him a while to get up the nerve to ask me how he could interview Castro and Guevara in Sierra Maestra. It was a question newsmen had asked me on more than one occasion, backing off fast as soon as they saw the difficulty of the undertaking. But Masetti, a staff member of the daily newspaper *El Mundo* and a free-lancer for the radio station of the same name, really seemed to have his mind made up. He didn't have an impressive professional background, and for that reason, to assure his future, he wanted a big news story. In February 1957 Herbert Matthews had shaken Cuba, as well as the rest of the world, with a series of three articles in *The New York Times* in which he revealed that Castro and his companions were alive. Those articles fascinated newsmen everywhere, especially in Latin America.

But Masetti's objective was, above all, political. Castro's rebellion had the unconditional support of Argentina's middle class, and this support had produced a dialectical response from the workers, who as a result began to favor Batista. Through oversimplified reasoning they associated Peron with Batista, since both men had military, if otherwise dissimilar, careers. Consequently, the names of General Aramburu and Admiral Rojas, both Argentines, were publicly linked with that of Fidel Castro, and since these were the men who had broken up the unions, jailed their leaders, and shot Peronista rebels, the working class came to identify the Cuban guerrilla with its national enemies.

Masetti was interested in finding out whether or not this interpretation of his fellow-Peronistas was correct.

One day he came to the La Paz café with his passport in one hand and his airplane ticket in the other. I couldn't help smiling: at last one of the newsmen was going through with it.

The repression in the Cuban cities had become savagely cruel in 1958. I told Masetti that I would give him only one address, a place where he could be put in touch with the underground university organization, and there he could ask to be taken to the mountains. Once in the mountains he could introduce himself with a letter addressed to Guevara, whom I hadn't seen since the latter part of 1955, when we said goodbye in Mexico. At first I thought of a long letter, full of personal news and political observations. But instead, I quickly wrote a short note, thinking that in the interest of Masetti's safety, it should be clear only to the addressee, and innocent-looking to the police. I wrote:

Dear Pig:
The bearer is a newspaperman and friend who wants to do a news program for *El Mundo* radio station in Buenos Aires. Please take good care of him, he's a good man.
Signed: The Sniper.

Masetti read those few lines and arched his brows. His introduction was certainly succinct.

Nevertheless, the address and the little note opened the way to Sierra Maestra. In March 1958 Masetti arrived at Fidel Castro's stronghold. He lived with the guerrillas for several weeks and discovered the simple friendliness of the men as well as the fierceness of the fighting. On his return he wrote:

I must confess that I left Buenos Aires full of doubts. My opinion

of Batista was already formed, of course. But I had to find out who
these people were who were trying to overthrow him, and where their
interests lay. We Argentines wanted to know who was behind the
Cuban revolution. We wanted to know if the bullets fired at Batista
were paid in dollars or rubles or pound sterling. Or if there had
cropped up in Latin America the bewildering exception of a revolution financed by its own people, a revolution on the road to victory.

His first contact with Castro, in a jungle clearing, convinced
him of how close the interrelationships were in Latin American
politics.

"Good evening," he said to Castro.

"Hello, how are you? How is Frondizi? Is he happy?" the
guerrilla leader asked.

By then Masetti had already met Ché. Here is his portrait of
him:

> He arrived on a mule, his legs hanging and the hump of his back
> apparently stretched between the barrels of a Beretta and a rifle with
> a telescopic sight, like two sticks holding up a large carcass. As the
> mule approached I could see a leather cartridge belt, heavy with
> ammunition, and a pistol hanging from his waist. Two magazines
> stuck out of his shirt pockets. A camera clung to his neck, and hairs
> trying to grow into a beard clung to his chin. He took his time dis-
> mounting, touching ground with enormous, muddied boots, and as
> he came toward me I figured that he measured about 5' 10", and
> that the asthma he suffered from couldn't be much of an obstacle to
> him. The famous Ché Guevara looked to me like a typical middle class
> Argentine, and somewhat like a rejuvenated caricature of Cantinflas.
> He invited me to have breakfast with him and we started eating,
> scarcely saying a word.

This cool encounter, however, soon began to warm up. Masetti
continued:

> Logically, the first questions came from him. And, logically too,
> they had to do with Argentine politics. My answers appeared to
> satisfy him, and after talking a short while, we realized that we agreed
> on many things and were not dangerous characters. We were soon
> talking quite freely—although we maintained a few reservations, as
> good Argentines of the same generation—and we began to use the
> familiar *tu*.

Masetti and Guevara were the same age: twenty-nine, only a few months apart.

Meeting Guevara was a decisive experience in Masetti's life, for it gave him a glimpse of his true calling as a revolutionary. Inside Masetti there was a leader of men, hidden these twenty-nine years but from then on trying only to emerge.

By the time he left the island, Masetti was already participating in the revolution. He made a trip to Caracas, where the Pact of the Parties that supported Castro in his final assault against the dictatorship was being worked out. In a mere three weeks he wrote a fifty-thousand-word article about the Cuban guerrillas, which he published in Buenos Aires in October 1958, when the fight on the island was entering its final phase.

In 1959 Guevara sent for Masetti and turned over to him the organization of the news agency *Prensa Latina*, whose role was to disseminate news about Cuba throughout the world, especially in Latin America. Masetti began to show great talent as an organizer, and by June of that year the news agency had a staff of over a hundred and fifty people, more than sixty of them in the central office in Havana. Branches were soon opened in almost every capital of the hemisphere, and there was even one in the United States.

This large journalistic enterprise was to run into as many obstacles as the number of consolidated positions it threatened. From the very beginning its fate was linked with that of the Cuban government, and as the Castro regime became isolated in the hemisphere, the agency saw its offices shut down and the dissemination of its news prohibited.

Toward the end of 1960 *Prensa Latina* still seemed to be holding its own. Masetti came to visit me at the Argentine Embassy in Bonn. We hadn't seen each other since his return from Cuba in July 1958, when he brought a record Guevara had made for his mother to confirm the fact, once and for all, that he was alive. In

those war days the news of Guevara's death in combat was
rumored frequently, although his family generally knew how
he was through an informant in Havana. This man was no other
than the Argentine ambassador in Cuba, Admiral Lynch, a first
cousin of Ché's father, whose mother's maiden name was also
Lynch.

In December 1960 Masetti was on a tour, stopping in Algiers
and probably destined for Moscow. But in Bonn he received instructions not to go on to the USSR, and he returned to Havana
shortly afterward. The next time I saw him, in his air-conditioned
offices in a tall building in Vedado, Havana's residential district,
Masetti was in a very nervous state, so much so that he was un-
intentionally rude to me. He immediately apologized. I haven't
the slightest doubt that his apology was sincere, because a short
time afterward, in April 1961, he had to resign from his post as
editor of *Prensa Latina*. He had had all kinds of problems, from
professional rivalry with Cuban newsmen who frowned on the
editorship of an Argentine, to political differences, especially
with veteran Communists, who usually got along well with Cuban
newsmen. Guevara backed him up as long as he could, but
Masetti's position became untenable. With Guevara's blessing,
Masetti resigned. Some weeks later, after the Bay of Pigs invasion, Masetti took part in a spectacular television panel in
which the principal captured invaders were interrogated. Masetti
was one of the journalists on the panel.

After that he slipped quietly into the background, but in 1963,
during my stay in Havana, he was close to Ché. Moreover, he
was present at many long conversations Guevara and I had, and
he seemed to be very knowledgable about a strategical theory
Guevara was perfecting at that time. He also seemed to be very
busy with his military training.

The theory was none other than the feasibility of bringing a nucleus of guerrillas into Argentine territory from a camp previously set up on Bolivian soil.

Guevara frequently repeated a quotation from José Marti: "Anyone who starts a war that can be avoided in a country is a criminal, as is anyone who does not start the inevitable war."

For Ché and Masetti the war in Argentina, the social revolution, was inevitable. It was only a matter of promoting it as efficiently as possible.

"We mustn't be afraid of violence," Guevara explained. "Violence is the midwife of the new societies. But it must be loosed at exactly the right moment, when the leaders of the people have found the most favorable conditions."

There were two subjective elements that he found of enormous importance. One was the awareness of the necessity for change, and the other was the conviction that this revolutionary change would come about. Both elements had to be joined with the objective conditions in each country, which in the case of Argentina appeared to be extremely favorable, as I have explained in the previous chapter. Guevara added to all these a firm desire to bring about the change and his conviction of the new interrelation of forces in the world. The result was an absolutely positive conclusion about the revolution's chances in Argentina.

Frankly, neither Masetti nor Ché ever mentioned in my presence the imminent attempt at a guerrilla campaign in Argentina. They showed a lively interest about conditions in that country, and the last time I was with them, in April 1963, the uprising by the Argentine navy convinced them that they were judging the situation correctly.

"A nucleus of guerrillas on any mountain, in a country with heavily populated cities," Guevara prophesied, "can be a permanent center of rebellion. It would be difficult for the repressive powers to liquidate quickly, or even in the course of years, guerrillas who have their social roots established in the territory, where that territory is favorable to guerrilla fighting, and where the people are acquainted with the tactics and strategy of guerrilla warfare."

Naturally, this theoretic plan could apply to Argentina. All that remained was to try to develop, with the plan in mind, a political situation in which the guerrillas could perform the role reserved for them.

Shortly after I left Havana, Masetti traveled secretly to South America to try out Guevara's plan.

In June 1963 Masetti was already in Bolivia. He had gone with three Cubans, all members of Ché's iron guard: Majors Hermes Peña Torres, Raúl Dávila, and "Papi."

When Masetti arrived in Bolivia, he already had two factors working against him. In May 1963 the leader of the peasant revolt in the valley of Cuzco, Peru, the student Hugo Blanco, had been thrown in prison and his movement had begun to deteriorate. This event upset plans for establishing a chain of guerrillas from Peru down to the north of Argentina, one of the most ambitious extensions of Guevara's revolutionary war. The other unexpected news was that the Argentine military, tired of wrangling among themselves, had decided to hand over national power to a civil government, chosen in fixed elections, though with some semblance of constitutional respect. These elections were to take place on July 7, 1963.

In other words, Masetti could not put much faith in the north—as he was warned by the emissaries of Hugo Blanco who came to see him in La Paz—and in the south there was the risk that a constitutional lull would set in, during which the ideal conditions for popular support to a guerrilla war would disappear.

"The economic powers," Guevara had said, "operate within a certain framework of legality, set up by themselves in order to have things their way. But when popular pressures grow, this middle class legality is violated by its own authors to check the momentum of the masses."

In Argentina, however, this process now appeared to be reversing itself. Those who had violated middle class legality preferred to return to it, in order to protect their interests. It was a period of transition, a bad time in which to pick the right course.

But Masetti had already picked his. The first men were beginning to arrive at the Emborozá Ranch in Bolivia, near the Argentine border. By a complicated recruiting system they were coming to join the "Ejército Guerrillero del Pueblo" (Peoples' Guerrilla Army), or EGP, as it would soon be called.

Apparently Masetti rejected any link or serious communication with the political organizations of Argentina. In doing this he clearly violated the Cuban model, since Fidel Castro had negotiated and made a pact with all the political parties and organizations ready to reach an understanding. Masetti was also violating one of the cardinal rules of the guerrilla movement by isolating his nucleus from collaboration with mass movements; Guevara himself had predicted that without mass support disaster would be inevitable.

Masetti preferred to look for help in two hotbeds of potential recruits: the university and the dissidents of the Communist Party. Both could supply him with men ready to risk their lives for revolutionary ideas. On the other hand, they were in no position to offer him an organization in the cities for sabotage or political agitation, not even a small one. His band of guerrillas, then, turned out to be a group of dedicated men, frequently of extraordinary quality, but completely separated from the social organizations of the country.

One day Federico Mendez—a mechanic, single, twenty-four years old—arrived at Emborozá. There were no more than four men camped with the leader of the guerrilla band, but it already had an emblem, a sun against a red and black background.

"Red," Masetti explained to Mendez, "stands for the blood of the revolution, and black is in mourning for the sufferings of the people."

Juan Jouvé—a student, single, twenty-three years old—also thought about the blood and the sufferings. He had been working at a trade school run by a religious order in the province of Córdoba, and had left his job on August 23, 1963. From there he went to Tarija, in Bolivia, where Hermes Peña, the Cuban, went to pick him up. Jouvé had a younger brother, Emilio, who also joined the band shortly afterward.

Masetti was surprised to learn that national elections had taken place in Argentina on July 7th, and that the Radical Party's candidate, Arturo Illia, a quiet country doctor, had won. The new president would take over the government in October, and for a while Masetti played with the hope that the military would not let him take office. If this happened, the many political and union organizations and other people who had lost all hope of establishing true democracy in Argentina would join forces. Before long they would clash with the usurping military, and then the repression would begin, followed by popular reaction; and then there would be more repression to quiet down the reaction. Between July and October the tiny guerrilla camp eagerly followed the course of events in Buenos Aires. But by the beginning of October it was clear that the military would hand over the government to Doctor Illia. Maseti realized that the Cuban example was not going to repeat itself, and instead of fighting against another dictator like Batista, he would have to face a modest civilian president, ready to compromise with the pressure groups in Argentina, and whose possible alternatives of government did not include violent repression.

Between September 20th and 25th, the small expedition crossed the border and passed into Argentine territory. Split into two groups, the guerrillas crossed the desert and waded the Bermejo

River, some ten miles from a small place called Aguas Blancas. They pitched their first camp near the Pescado River, and Masetti immediately prepared a political letter asking the new president to resign, to admit that his election had been the product of an illegal compromise and was essentially anti-democratic, since the majority force, the Peronistas, had not been able to vote for their own candidates.

Masetti's letter, signed "Major Segundo," was published in Buenos Aires in *Compañero*, a weekly put out by the Peronist Left wing. It had a limited impact on political circles of the Left, for *Compañero* bore no resemblance to those media which Castro had at his disposal when he rebelled against Batista, such as the magazine *Bohemia*, which had the biggest circulation in Cuba at the time. Masetti's voice came out in the weekly as a mere squeak.

But the letter did alert the military secret services and the police, who decided to set up a regular watch to check on the strength of the guerrilla force. And it managed to fire the imagination of several dozen young men, who set out for the north.

Masetti had composed a disciplinary code for his men, to punish misdemeanors and crimes. Sentences ran from extra duty in camp to a cut-down in rations and, in extreme cases, the death penalty. His fellow conspirators called him the Second (Segundo), which, more than a pseudonym, signified the existence of a First Major. This, of course, was Ché.

Degrees of optimism among the guerrillas varied, but Masetti must certainly have felt lower than the others. He had come into Argentina to light the fuse for a long political and social crisis, and had been out-maneuvered by events, by the coming to power of an inoffensive man whom he could not in any sense accuse of being a dictator. The fact was, Masetti was a trapped man, and no doubt the heaviest burden of all was that he did not want to free himself of his promises to Guevara (had he wanted an excuse to do so, he could reasonably have fallen back on the unfavorable swing in the political situation).

Life in the jungle, first in Bolivia and later in Salta, was much harder than the men had expected. Masetti's Cuban companions, veteran campaigners, noticed the difference here in a wild fruit, similar to the *malanga*, which in the Cuban countryside was an abundant source of wild nourishment. In the Argentine jungle this similar fruit turned out to be toxic, and when they ate it they suffered horrible convulsions. Some were affected by it for life.

Unfavorable political conditions and the material problems of survival played on the nerves of the small expedition. Far from their homes, several of them thousands of miles away, the guerrillas bogged down in despair. The most affected seemed to be a twenty-year-old recruit, Adolfo Rotblat, nicknamed "Pupi," who was harrassed by continual attacks of asthma. "Pupi's" case became an additional hardship for the guerrillas, as all their exercises, marches, and work were hampered by his physical frailty. At last, he decided to desert.

"Pupi's" intentions were soon known, and they became a catalyst for the overall moral crisis of the expedition. There were no enemies in sight, yet one of their own who had sworn to stand by the revolutionary code wanted to desert them. A tribunal was formed to judge "Pupi" and condemned him to death. An entry in Hermes' diary records the execution, and what led up to it, in a few words.

The crossing of the border had been called "Operation Golden." That was in September. In December Masetti ordered his men to carry out the second part of his plan, which he called "Operation Spring-board" and which consisted of bringing in the arms still stored in Bolivia. Six men went to recover the weapons. They found them distributed in suitcases along the route between Bermejo and Tarija.

A few more volunteers arrived: a twenty-three-year-old brick-layer with one eye missing who, because of his physical defect, was excluded as a fighter but taken on as cook. A philosophy student, twenty-seven, from a prosperous family, whose maternal grandfather, an admiral, had been Police Commissioner in Buenos Aires twenty-three years before. Another student, twenty-five, recently married. Two brothers, unemployed mechanics, who came to the camp together. Two employees from the Israelite Bank in Córdoba, who had been militant Communists but preferred armed fighting to politics and arrived full of enthusiasm, so much so that one of them, Groswald, had his toenails extracted to avoid being handicapped by ingrown nails during the jungle marches. An oil driller without a job, twenty-nine. A flower vendor, twenty. A medical student, twenty-two, who had deserted from the army. A Galician, nineteen, born in Vigo, Spain. And a Merchant Marine who had just had his twenty-fifth birthday.

This heterogeneous troop received its military instruction from Major Hermes. Meanwhile, Masetti brooded. There was no turning back for him, not so much because of the events up to then, but because his conscience wouldn't let him admit political defeat. He couldn't disband his men before they had fought, and he couldn't find anyone to fight against. His neurosis grew, he retreated into himself more and more each day.

On February 19, 1964, the expedition's underlying moral crisis again turned the guerrillas against themselves. Groswald, nicknamed "Nardo," was tried for a series of offenses: insubordination, decline of revolutionary morale, and carelessness with arms and war material. Captain Hermes presided over a tribunal that deliberated for three hours in the middle of the jungle on the sentence "Nardo" deserved. The court was undecided. But Masetti added the weight of his opinion, and Groswald too was inexplicably condemned to death.

This boy, who was only nineteen, asked to be shot wearing his guerrilla uniform, his black beret, his jackboots, his leather belt, and his light green sunglasses. As he listened to the sentence, sweat slid down his forehead. He dried it with a brown-bordered white handkerchief he had bought a few days before coming up to the mountains. He faced his companions with decision and promised to die with dignity. Three guerrillas fired at him, and two bullets entered his body, around the fourth and fifth ribs. Captain Hermes finished him off with his Luger: the bullet entered his right cheek bone and came out through the back of his neck.

Was this the guerrilla war with which Masetti and Guevara had dreamed of shaking Argentina? "Major Segundo" knew it was not. Yet he was trying, so far without success, to find some way to reach the masses, the instrument needed to break down the isolation in which he found himself. This isolation had become a terrible psychological threat which grew worse when they found they could not establish radio contact with the outside world. A transmitter which they had intended to use for communication with the outside, as far away as Havana, had quickly proved inoperative.

Meanwhile, the military intelligence service had sent out two of its men to infiltrate the guerrilla movement. One, a chiropodist, passed himself off as a Peronista, ready to do anything to overthrow the government. He introduced himself to some young recruits who were getting ready to travel to Salta and had them meet a friend, as resolute as he. On March 2nd, when they got to the first guerrilla camp, one of the Cubans received them and welcomed them to the People's Guerrilla Army. But they had hardly been issued weapons and started for the main camp when the two intruders provoked an incident, and one of them shot the guerrilla at the head of the column, wounding him in the leg.

From that moment on the guerrilla band could consider itself discovered and closely pursued. In the next few days several guerrillas were surrounded by the gendarmery, a militarized police force that watched the borders and was assigned to wipe out the EGP. The guerrillas' supplies were cut off, and as the ring slowly tightened around them, hunger began to take its toll. Three died of starvation after trying to subsist on a diet of wild vegetables. Another was surprised by the gendarmes in a treetop where he had had to take refuge from the claws of two jaguars.

In mid-April Major Hermes and a companion surprised an advance guard of the gendarmery and killed one of the soldiers. It was the only real skirmish of the Argentine guerrilla war. The gendarmes spotted Hermes almost immediately and surrounded him. He managed to fire twenty-eight bullets with his automatic carbine, and his companion shot four of the six bullets in his Smith & Wesson .38 before they were both killed.

By then fourteen men had been captured by the gendarmes, who tortured and humiliated them in a vicious manner. Five of them were submerged in the viscera of the dead men and were dragged by the hair amidst laughter and mortal threats.

In the meantime Masetti had interned himself in the thick jungle of Yuto, a hell of vegetation and wild animals where the plant life was so thick that it was possible to walk for days without seeing the sun. He never returned; no one ever heard from him again. The jungle swallowed him.

That is the story of the guerrilla war in Argentina, as Guevara himself learned it at the end of 1964. Another very good friend of Ché's, the lawyer, Gustavo Roca, as well as other lawyers from the province, including myself, took on the defense of the guerrilla prisoners in Salta. From their declarations and confidences about all their painful experiences, we got a complete picture of this tragic and catastrophic guerrilla expedition.

What were Ché's conclusions? It's hard to guess. Roca, who met him in Paris at the beginning of 1965, noted above all that Guevara was overcome by tremendous grief for his two good friends, Masetti and Hermes. They had died as brave men, they had lived up to his ideas, up to his exacting standard. Their noble courage had demanded its reward: death. But what political conclusion, what answer to his nucleus theory, what analysis of failure, was there in all this?

The answer would be two years in coming. And Ché himself would give it to the world.

8

The Burning Mystery

The tragedy of "Major Segundo" in the mountains and jungles of northern Argentina was the quietest guerrilla defeat in Latin America. It received little publicity from the press, with even the leftist publications afraid to involve themselves in an adventure that many saw as a provocation organized by the intelligence services. This suspicion was unfounded—except in the case of the two spies who easily infiltrated the guerrilla group—but the fact remained that the huge masses of the industrial urban suburbs got to know almost nothing about the guerrilla army forming up north. And the peasants, to whom the rebel message was in general addressed, learned even less.

"In getting a foothold in the countryside," Guevara had written, "a guerrilla band that attaches itself to the peasant masses will grow from a minor to a major group, it will destroy the army in a head-on fight, and from the countryside will go on to take over the cities."

Masetti had been faithful to this idea. And yet, at the end of ten hard months in the most inhospitable terrain one can imagine, his forces numbered fewer than thirty men, isolated and pun-

163

ished with neurosis and despair. Masetti's own overwhelming conclusion was that the peasant masses could not join him, nor he
them, simply because there were no such masses in the north of
Argentina. The density of the population is generally sparse in
Argentina, particularly in the northern countryside. Concentration
of some importance exists in timber lands and in areas where
sugar and cotton is cultivated, but these are islands in the middle
of thinly populated wastes, barren or overrun by wild plant life.
Masetti should have appealed to the politically important masses
in the industrial districts, but he was a stranger there. His message
would have generated only mistrust.

This suggests another point on which the Cuban model proved
superior to the Argentine experience, for Fidel Castro was a well-
known personality on the island before the *Granma* expedition.
He had run for deputy in Prío Socarrás' party and had been a
prominent agitator at the university. He had attended an aristocratic high school where he had made friends who, at the time
he turned rebel, were beginning to run the best known and most
influential businesses and law firms in Cuba. Not only was
Masetti a virtual unknown, his name wasn't familiar even to
most of his fellow journalists. His career had grown outside Argentina, and he lacked friends or solid political ties in his own country. For ten months he traveled all over the south of Bolivia and
the north of Argentina with considerable ease. He and his followers had arrived from Cuba in a roundabout way, but traveling
like anybody else, and were able to cross borders without arousing
suspicion. It was only because the guerrilla band sent a public
letter to the Argentine government that the Internal Security
Services took notice of its existence.

No doubt this was one lesson Guevara should have learned
from Masetti's tragedy. And yet, he introduced no notable modifi-
cations in the main lines of his own strategy.

Why?

It is difficult to explain through any single motive. I shall try to put together the combination of reasons that led Guevara to repeat Masetti's error almost mechanically and with remarkably similar results.

One point that immediately comes up in any analysis of Guevara's motivations in pursuing guerrilla warfare in South America is his personal position in Cuba and his particular relationship with Fidel Castro.

The industrialization of Cuba—technically a developed country—as outlined by Guevara's four-year plan in 1961, could be considered a failure in the beginning of 1964. All the defects in organization and specialization that can plague an industrialized country during its development inexorably showed up in Cuba. Factories were built in places where water, electricity, and roads were insufficient. Sometimes there was a shortage of labor, and in general, technicians had to be improvised. There were appreciable shifts in population, since industrial work has a fascinating drawing power in agricultural countries; accordingly, while the organization of industries was still being worked out, the countryside was disorganized. In some areas there were large losses of laborers, and in others production fell off because of sudden readjustments in the labor force. The movement to put Cuba on its feet industrially caused as many inconveniences in a very short time as were experienced in Argentina or Brazil through the forties and fifties. It is amazing that the industralizers in Cuba received the same advice from the Soviet Union that that Argentina and Brazil had received from the United States: that for economic reasons agricultural countries should not try to become industrialized, but rather should reap the benefits of high quality manufacture from industrial nations. In Cuba's case the Russians also found justification in the reduced size of that country's internal market and in the conspicuous fact that it had no chance to export its manufacture to any of its neighbors. This political and economic isolation forced it to depend on other markets, and these, whether the Soviet Union and European socialist countries or the capitalist countries of Europe, could buy only agricultural products from Cuba.

Therefore, Guevara's plan had to rely on Soviet indulgence for a longer period than he had counted on. Yet Cuban industrialization had to have an export market, and in order to obtain it other nations of Central and South America would have to adopt a regime similar to Cuba's. In this event there would be a clash between the United States and the USSR—since the USSR had guaranteed that Cuba would not try to expand politically—and, consequently, Moscow's indulgence would end and, with it, the industrialization program and its heavy financing.

Toward the end of 1964 Castro consented to Cuba being pigeonhold in the socialist world's great distribution of work. But Guevara did not agree.

"An agricultural Cuba, once more the sugar mill of the world," he had told me one day in 1963, "would cast doubt on the survival of socialism. In addition, she would be so internationally weak, she would be dependent on Soviet protection for her life. And the revolution wasn't fought for that."

The fact was, there couldn't be a revolution without industrialization, and there couldn't be industries without markets. To obtain markets the revolution would have to continue in Latin America, in which case the United States would call the USSR to task, and if Cuba did not listen to the USSR, the latter would end her commitment to the Cuban socialist regime. That, of course, would mean the end of the revolution. Everyone knew that only the immense military strength of Russia could balance that of the United States and prevent a devastating attack from the north. An inflexible vicious circle.

In March 1964 Ché traveled to Geneva at the head of the Cuban delegation to the World Conference on Trade and Devel-

opment. He emphasized the danger of foreign capital investments
to world trade and peace, for they would end up dominating
national economies from within. He also proposed that as long as
the underdeveloped countries could not obtain equitable prices
for their products, the payment of dividends, interests, and amor-
tizations should be suspended by common agreement.

When the conference ended, he spent two days in Paris and
then went to Algiers, where his relations with Ben Bella flourished.
As a result of this trip the Algerian president appealed to the
United States, a few months later, for a normalization of relations
between Washington and Havana.

"I can't understand," Ben Bella said, "how the United States
can be willing to maintain direct telephone communication with
the Kremlin and at the same time oppose the Cuban people's right
to choose the form of government that suits them best."

In November 1964 Guevara set out once more, this time for
Moscow. It was his third visit to the USSR, but on this tour he
would make a real pilgrimage to many parts of the world, a trip
lasting more than four months.

His visit to the Soviet Union was, no doubt, the key to his later
profound differences with Castro. The idea definitely grew in
him that the Russians were contemplating an actual coexistence
with the United States, signifying, in the first place, the division
of the world into two areas to be respected by both powers, and
in the second place, the distribution of work among the nations
of each area. For Cuba this meant an agricultural future and a
weak position as a world nation.

His discussions with the Soviets came out in the open in his
speech on December 11, 1964, before the General Assembly of
the United Nations. He had arrived in New York unexpectedly
with the Cuban delegation, and some people thought he was also
speaking for the Algerian president, Ben Bella.

"American imperialism," he said then, "has attempted to make others believe that peaceful coexistence is for the exclusive use of the great global powers. But," he emphasized, "there cannot be peaceful coexistence between the powerful only, if world peace is to be assured. Peaceful coexistence must be carried out between all nations, regardless of size, of their previous historical ties, and of the problems that may arise between them from time to time."

That same week Guevara appeared on television in New York on the CBS program *Face the Nation*.

"All Cuba wants is to be left alone by the United States," he exclaimed, "for better or for worse."

And then he went on to show that his discussions in Moscow were weighing on his mind. He admitted the errors in his industrialization plan, promising to correct them, and he said that harmonious relations with the United States would be "very good" for Cuba. Out in the street a picket-line of anti-Castristas booed him, but he looked right through them.

On December 17th he left New York for Algiers, via Canada, and renewed his conversations with Ben Bella, reinforcing the impression that an independent socialist axis was in the making between Cuba and Algiers. On Christmas Day he flew to Bamako, in Mali, and again his speeches took on a fiery tone.

"The revolutionary fight against United States' intervention," he said, "is assuming an increasingly continental character in the hemisphere."

It was on this tour, to which other countries were quickly added, that Ché became, in effect, the traveling agent for the revolution of the Third World. The trip had the implicit backing of Ben Bella, who, in Africa, stood for the Algerian revolution, the hardest fought and most hopeful revolution of the great black continent.

In Brazzaville, the Congo, he was received at the beginning of January 1965 by President Alphonse Massemba-Debat, with whom he discussed the state of the anti-imperialist struggle in Africa. Soon after that he went on to Conakry, Guinea, and to Accra, Ghana.

This tour could only mean that he was sounding out the African governments on the possibility of a political union under the leadership of Algiers.

In Ghana Guevara was momentarily distracted by his old interest: one day he traveled eighteen miles from the capital to the Botanical Garden of Aburi, and enjoyed himself observing the varieties of African flora assembled there. It was a child's dream come true. He also traveled to the Volta River, where a gigantic dam was under construction, and there he spoke about wars of liberation:

"There have been many experiences in armed conflict in Colombia, Venezuela, and Guatemala. Everywhere there are accounts of failure, and these should be made known so that profitable lessons may be drawn for the struggle of the future."

At the end of that month his visit to Dahomey was announced. But before leaving Ghana, Ché visited a worker brigade camp, where he was given a *kente*, the traditional costume for formal occasions, which he accepted happily.

From Dahomey his next jump was back to Algiers, where he compared notes with the leaders of the revolution, and from there, Paris.

One of his oldest and most loyal friends, Gustavo Roca, the Argentine lawyer, was waiting for him in Paris. Roca had been a high school friend of Ché's in Córdoba, Argentina, and he had visited him several times in Cuba. Their meeting this time was a sad occasion: Roca was bringing Guevara the complete report on Masetti's guerrilla band, including the résumé of the prisoners' declarations and the confirmation that Masetti and Hermes Peña were dead. It was a defeat for Latin American revolution, but Guevara took it as a personal defeat.

Early in February he went to Dar Es Salaam, Tanzania, and delivered a speech in which he disclosed the real meaning of his unprecedented African tour:

"After completing my tour through seven African countries," he said, "I am convinced a common fight is possible against colonialism, imperialism, and neocolonialism."

On February 19th Ché flew to Cairo. There he again ran into the leader of the Congo rebellion, Gaston Soumialot, whom he had met two years before on an airplane flight across Africa. Soumialot was a peasant, forty-five years old, who had spent fourteen years fighting for the nationalist cause in the Congo. He was a legend. They said he belonged to the same tribe as Lumumba, but this was not true. It was true, however, that he had accompanied Lumumba on his political campaigns, that he was one of the most successful agitators in his country, and that he had spent several of his last years in various prisons. In September 1964 Soumialot had proclaimed a Popular Republic of the Congo, with its capital in Stanleyville, and had taken the post of Defense Minister in its government.

Soumialot went back and forth to Cairo, where the Congo's revolutionary government had a headquarters in the Zamalek neighborhood, the city's diplomatic district. There the Supreme Court of the Revolution met under the direction of a committee presided over by Soumialot. His two vice-presidents were Pierre Mulele and Laurent Kabila. Mulele was the man directing the armed struggle in the Leopoldville and Kasai zone, while Kabila was the head of the insurrection in Katanga and Kivu. Both men held concepts of guerrilla warfare very much like Guevara's: since they lacked political cadres in the cities, their plan was to create a real army in the countryside. The cities would fall in due time.

Guevara felt genuine sympathy for the African revolution, and had taken Patrice Lumumba's assassination in January 1961 as more than just a political loss. The Cuban revolutionaries had turned Lumumba's name into a symbol, a figure whose long-suffering face and career became known over the entire island.

Guevara and Soumialot exchanged invitations: for Soumialot to visit and learn about Cuba, where the revolution was in power, and for Guevara to fight in the Congo, where the revolution was still a dream and where the political picture was complicated by fragmentation and tribal resistance.

On February 24, 1965, Guevara took part in the sessions of the Second Afro-Asiatic Economic Seminar meeting in Algiers. He defended Cuba's right to speak at a reunion of African and Asiatic peoples, affirming that:

". . . the attack of American imperialism against Viet Nam or the Congo must be answered by supplying those brother countries with all the instruments of defense they need and by giving them all our unconditional support."

He returned to Cairo at the beginning of March 1965 and resumed his conversations with the Congolese rebels. He noticed there were disagreements among them that revealed, deep down, the hidden differences between the Chinese and the Russians about what tactics to apply in Africa. Nasser invited him to visit the construction of the Aswan Dam, a marvel of Soviet engineering in conjunction with Arab labor. It was the last stop of his long tour.

He returned to Havana on March 14th, and received a simple welcome, although met by the top government staff: Fidel Castro, President Osvaldo Dorticós, political leaders Carlos Rafael Rodríguez and Emilio Aragonés, and several ministers. Also on hand were his wife, who was expecting a baby, and his friend Roca, who barely managed to greet him as Guevara was rushed off in Castro's car.

It was not until two days later that Roca was able to get together with Guevara. Ché explained that he had been talking with Castro for close to forty hours. He had given him a long oral report. Had they quarreled? Guevara didn't say.

He switched the talk to something else. He asked Roca to notify Hermes Peña's father, an old peasant, about his son's death far away in Argentina. Roca agreed, but then quickly backed down, admitting he didn't have the courage. Guevara said he would do it himself.

Roca was leaving soon to return to Argentina, and Ché said that he would give him a letter for his mother in Buenos Aires.

Guevara announced to his mother that he was prepared to leave the leadership of the Cuban revolution, that after working for thirty days cutting cane he would spend five years in a factory to study on the spot the functioning of one of the many industries he had directed from the top.

Did he really plan to do this?

Perhaps.

Ché's relation with his mother was not in the least conventional. It had always been full of complicities: Celia was a good companion, physically weakened by asthma like Ché, her outlook shaped, like his, by rebellion and the political literature of the Left.

Toward the end of the letter he wrote what may serve as an important clue in analyzing this darkest and most crucial period in his life. He told her that she must not travel to Cuba for any reason whatever.

Was he afraid of something? Had he decided then to leave the country in spite of the fact that, a few lines back in the letter, he had said that he would stay to cut cane and manage factories?

Ché's letter, written on March 16, 1965, was delivered by Roca after his trip to Europe on April 13th.

When she received it, Celia invited me to her house and asked me to read it. For many years this had been our habit with Ché's letters. I was as confused as she. She had herself under control quickly and asked me if I knew of some confidential courier who could take her answer to Havana personally. At that time there was a union leader about to leave for Cuba on an invitation to the May Day celebration. I told her I'd give it to him and she agreed. Then she sat down to write a letter. Its text, published for the first time, follows:

Buenos Aires, April 14, 1965

My dear one:

Do my letters sound strange to you? I don't know if we have lost the naturalness with which we used to speak to each other, or if we never had it and have always spoken with that slightly ironic tone used by those of us from the shores of the Plate, exaggerated by our own private family code.

The fact is that anxiety has always made me abandon my ironic tone and be straightforward. Apparently that's when my letters are not understood and become strange and enigmatic.

Since we have adopted this diplomatic tone in our correspondence, I too have to read hidden meanings between the lines and try to interpret them. I've read your last letter the way I read the news published in *La Prensa* or *La Nacion* of Buenos Aires, solving, or trying to, the real meanings and the full implication of every phrase.

The result has been a sea of confusion, and even greater anxiety and alarm.

I'm not going to use diplomatic language. I'm going straight to the point. It seems to me true madness that, with so few heads in Cuba with ability to organize, you should all go cut cane for a month, as your main job, when there are so many and such good cane cutters among the people. Doing it as volunteer work, during times normally given to rest or recreation, a Saturday or a Sunday, makes some kind of sense. Doing it as a full time job also makes sense, when you're trying to demonstrate conclusively the advantage and necessity of using machinery to cut cane, since Cuba's foreign currency will rely on, or come from, the harvest and number of tons obtained.

A month is a long time. There must be reasons I don't know. Speaking now of your own case, if, after that month, you're going to dedicate yourself to the management of a factory, a job successfully performed by Castellanos and Villegas, it seems to me that the madness has turned to absurdity, especially if this job is to take five years, to give you a true picture.

Since I know that you try not to miss a single day at your Ministry, when I saw your trip abroad dragging on so long, I asked myself: will Ernesto go on being Minister of Industries when he returns to Cuba? Who has given approval, who has the authority in this dispute that has led to your decision?

These questions have been partially answered. If you're going to manage a factory, it's because you're no longer Minister. Depending on who is named in your place, I'll know if the dispute has been settled in a reasonable way. At any rate, your managing a factory for five years is too big a waste of your ability. And this is not your mother speaking. It's an old woman who hopes to see the whole world converted to socialism. I believe that, if you go through with this, you will not be giving your best service to the cause of world socialism.

If all roads in Cuba have been closed to you, for whatever reason, in Algiers there's a Mr. Ben Bella who would appreciate your organizing his economy, or advising him on it; or a Mr. Nkrumah in Ghana who would welcome the same help. Yes, you'll always be a foreigner. That seems to be your permanent fate.

What a letter! It's a bore! I feel like tearing it up, but I'm going to send it anyway. I was thrilled to receive the family photos. They're all delightful, though I don't see your face or expression in any of your children. I'm happy to know Aleida came through all right, since I was very worried about her during her pregnancy with this last baby.

Both G. and J. rave about the beauty of your secret love. I'd have liked to see her in a photograph too. She is such an exotic type and has such Oriental charm and gentleness that she could compete in beauty with Florencia, Roberto's oldest daughter—which, I assure you, is saying a lot.

J. told me that you tried to give him some news about me and were left with your mouth open, because he already knew everything from me—I'm one up on you! Both he and G. are very impressed by the long step Cuba has taken towards organization.

Passing to another subject, I think I told you that Luis and Celia have separated. Luis wanted to go to Cuba to work there. He's a talented man. But he's a bit wary right now because he's not sure how things will turn out. Juan Martín has another brand new boy who isn't a month old yet.

Yes, I'm very sorry I can't travel to Cuba now and be with you, even if only to say to you, "Good morning" or "ciao." Repeated day after day, this takes on a certain value. I'd also have liked to know little Celia and little Ernesto and to listen to Aliucha's chatter. Some other time.

I don't believe any clown is going to blow up the world. Although, the things those brutes, the Americans do, scare the living you-know-what out of me. I believe there will be some clowns left, and they will somehow reconstruct a more just society, even if they have to start all over with bows and arrows and tribal groups.

A hug, a great big hug for you and yours.

CELIA.

P.S. Don't forget to embrace Eliseo for me. A problem of conscience has cropped up with the *Cuban Geology* you sent me for Dr. Catalano, because it so happens that Dr. Catalano has an important post in Illia's government in the Bureau of Mines and a Christian-Democrat niece who leads him around by the nose. Maybe I ought to do what Beethoven did with Napoleon, to whom he had dedicated his Third Symphony and then, when he could no longer have it dedicated to him, he inscribed it:
"To the great man you once were."

Celia's letter to her son was to follow a strange, almost magical course. Written with deep preoccupation, it also marked Celia's final physical decline. That midnight, when she came down to open the door of the old house where she lived, she could hardly make it back up the stairs. Although she leaned on my arm, I practically carried her. I scolded her for not seeing a doctor, but she said it was just fatigue. Actually, Celia had lived with the threat of cancer for almost twenty years, ever since they had operated on one of her breasts, affected by a malignant tumor. The operation had upset Guevara very much. He was beginning to study medicine, and, with a mixture of ingenuous filial love and a spirit of investigation, he set up a small laboratory at home, where he experimented for weeks with guinea pigs, using petroleum-based solutions.

Cancer was now making its final attack on Ché's mother. And so was fate. For the union leader who was to leave with the letter was suddenly taken off the list of those invited by the Cuban government. He was a Peronista, and these invitations were checked at the last minute by the Communist Party of Argentina, which in many cases vetoed them. This was one of those cases.

On April 30th Fidel Castro went to cut cane, as did the other revolutionary leaders, and he granted an informal interview to several foreign newsmen. They all wanted to know where Ché was. His disappearance from public ceremonies and from his ministerial office was the talk of the whole of Cuba, and news of it was beginning to leak out of the country.

"The only thing I can tell you," Castro explained, "is that Major Guevara will always be where he is most useful to the revolution. I think his tour of Africa was very fruitful. He was also in China on a visit with one of our delegations. He has many faces and an extraordinary understanding. One of our best all-around leaders."

This declaration, coming after a month of silence, heightened the curiosity about Ché's whereabouts. A newspaper account saying that Guevara would reappear on May Day in the traditional parade of the masses turned out to be false.

On May 10th Celia's condition became very serious, and she was interned in the Stapler Sanatorium, in the aristocrat section north of Buenos Aires; a few days later her family was politely asked to remove her. The owners of the sanatorium insisted that the presence of the mother of a Communist leader could ruin their business reputation.

About this time the union man who was to take the letter to Havana returned it to me, his trip having been cancelled. I notified Celia about this unlucky turn, and she asked me to hold onto the letter until I found a new messenger.

On May 16th the doctors decided that Celia's death was imminent. I telephoned Havana, and Aleida answered. She seemed very confused. Guevara was not in Havana, but he was in Cuba. I explained that his mother had only a few hours left to live and that some way ought to be found to let him know. She didn't think it would be easy, but I explained to her that, wherever Guevara was, he should be reachable by telephone or radio.

On the 18th Aleida made a long-distance call to the sanatorium. Celia was in a near coma, but she sat up in bed as if an electric shock had run through her. It was a frustrating conversation, with a great deal of shouting and a sense of hopelessness. At noon, I sent a cable:

Major Ernesto Guevara, Ministry of Industries. Havana.
Your mother very ill wants to see you. Your friend embraces
you.   Ricardo Rojo.

This cable didn't get an answer either, and on May 19th Ceila de la Serna de Guevara died.

I was one of the three funeral speakers at Celia's burial. The three of us, as well as many common friends and relatives, questioned one another with our eyes:

Where the hell is Ché?

For Guevara not to have answered his mother's final call, he simply could not have known what was happening. Aleida said he was in Cuba, and there was no reason to suppose she was lying. But where? In a place where there was no telephone. But on May 21st the Havana newspapers published the news of Ché's mother's death. He continued to ignore it. Evidently, besides not having a telephone, he was where no newspapers were available.

I believe Guevara was in reclusion, though not a prisoner. This reclusion was an act of political discipline. It implied a long session of self-criticism, undertaken voluntarily. And it also answered the last question in his mother's letter: "Who has given approval, who has the authority in this dispute that has led to your decision?"

The rules of this reclusion would seem to have been set down by Guevara himself, or in any case they had been agreed to with Castro in a way so strict that they were not broken for a reason as important as his mother's death.

In April 1959, following Castro's trip through the United States, Ché had gone through a similar experience. He thought Castro would compromise the course of the revolution by trusting the United States. He frankly told him so and immediately retired to his house with his iron guard. While Castro worked out the problem, Guevara and his friends remained confined and came out only when the head of the revolutionary government renounced his temptation.

What are we to make of that episode? Was he a prisoner, or was he exercising his tenacity to win him a political victory? Was his silence of 1965 owed to a similar situation?

From the information I have, Ché's reclusion lasted from March 20th to the end of July 1965, when he left Cuba for the Congo via Cairo.

In June, while Guevara was still in self-imposed isolation, the leader of the Algerian revolution was overthrown. Ben Bella's fall shook the Cuban regime and instigated an urgent revision of the entire diplomacy of African alliances which Guevara had built up in his fiery tour at the beginning of the year. As the Cubans saw it, the African revolution was going under, torpedoed by neocolonialism and anarchy. Guevara assumed the grave responsibility of going to the center of the black continent to collaborate personally in the Congo rebellion and keep the revolution afloat.

This Algerian event was of basic importance to Guevara as he developed his political analysis in isolation from the rest of the world. It should be weighed along with the letters Fidel Castro made known on October 3rd of that year, in which Guevara gave up his Cuban citizenship, his post as Minister, and his Major's rank.

These letters, according to Castro, were delivered to him by Guevara on April 1st.

"The date was not inserted," Castro declared on October 3rd, "because the letter was not to be read until the moment was considered opportune; but, to be specific, it was delivered on April First of this year, exactly six months and two days ago."

Although many doubted this statement by the leader of the Cuban revolution, it was unquestionably accurate. This can be seen from another letter, addressed to Guevara's parents. It too was not dated at the time of writing, but the fact that Guevara addressed it in the plural, to both parents, shows that he wrote it before his mother's death on May 20th.

In a way, the three letters signify an end to the most rigorous period of Ché's self-criticism, from March 17th to April 30, 1965.

What does the balance-sheet of this period show, a period of political revision in which Castro and Ché discussed each point under dispute?

A reading of the letters reveals that Guevara changed his mind about starting at the bottom by working in the cane fields and managing factories. Castro convinced him that this behavior would expose the conflict that had broken out between the two of them. Faced by his own standards of revolutionary leadership, Ché, like the old-time Bolsheviks, preferred to resign before voluntarily converting himself into an antagonist of the socialist government. He was a step away from becoming another Trotsky, but he had learned something from a careful reading of the reflections of other Bolshevik contempories of Trotsky: when the revolutionary government's fate is at stake, individual points of view must take second place.

Guevara realized that he must not hurt Fidel Castro's stature as ruler; he had to support him most now that their differences had reached a point of open conflict. He also understood that he could not remain on the island, stripped of his responsibilities, because this would be a big blow to the international standing of the revolution. There was nothing to do but leave. It was only a matter of choosing the right moment.

Ché's letter to Fidel Castro follows:

Havana
Year of the agriculture

Fidel:

At this hour I remember many things, when I met you in Maria Antonia's house, when you urged me to join you, all the tensions and preparations.

One day someone came by to ask who should be notified in case of death, and the real possibility struck us all. We realized later it was true, that in a revolution you triumph or die (if it's a true revolution). Many companions were left along the road to victory.

Today everything seems less dramatic because we have matured, but things repeat themselves. I feel I've carried out that part of my duty that bound me to the Cuban revolution in its own land, and I'm saying goodbye to you, to my friends, to your people, who are now mine.

I formally resign from my duties in the party leadership, from my post as minister, from my rank as major, from my Cuban citizenship. Nothing legal binds me to Cuba, only ties of a kind that can't be broken like official appointments.

Looking back over my life, I believe I have worked with sufficient honesty and dedication to consolidate the triumph of the revolution. My only serious fault is not to have trusted you more, from the first moments in Sierra Maestra, and not to have understood quickly enough your qualities as leader and revolutionary. I have lived through marvellous days and, at your side, I felt the pride of belonging to our people during the bright and sad days of the Caribbean crisis. There has seldom been a more brilliant statesman than you during those days. I am also proud of having followed you without hesitating, identifying myself with your way of thinking and seeing and appreciating dangers (and principles).

Other lands claim the help of my modest efforts. I can do what you can't, because of your responsibilities at the helm of Cuba, and the time has come for us to separate.

Let it be known that I do so with a mixture of happiness and pain. Here I am leaving my purest hopes as a builder and the dearest of those who are dear to me . . . and I am leaving a people that accepted me as a son. This tears part of my spirit. To the new battlefields I shall carry the faith you taught me, the feeling that I am fulfilling the most sacred duty: fighting against imperialism, wherever it is. This is a source of comfort and more than heals any wound.

I say once more that I free Cuba of any responsibility, except that which stems from its example. If the hour of reckoning comes to me under other skies, may my last thought be for this people and espe cially for you. I thank you for your teachings and your example, and I'll try to be faithful whatever may happen to me. I have always identified myself with the foreign policies of the revolution, and I still do. Wherever I end up I'll feel the responsibility of being a Cuban revolutionary and will act as one. I am leaving nothing material for my children and my wife and it doesn't sadden me. I am glad it's so. I ask nothing for them; the state will give them enough to live on and to receive an education.

I have many things to say to you and our people, but I feel that they're not necessary. Words can't express what I want to say, and there's no sense wasting paper with my scribbles. Until victory, always. Country or death.

I embrace you with complete revolutionary zeal.

CHÉ

The other two letters, one for his parents and the other for his children, reveal Ché's complex personality, the love for his parents he had never quite expressed, and a tenderness toward his children, its expression hampered by his political work and his trips outside Cuba.

Here are the texts of these letters:

To my parents
Dear Folks:

Once more I feel Rocinante's ribs under my heels; I'm taking to the road again with my shield on my arm.

Almost ten years ago, I wrote you another farewell letter. If I re member right, I regretted that I wasn't a better soldier and a better doctor; I'm not interested in the second any more, and I'm not such a bad soldier.

Essentially, nothing has changed, except that I am much more conscientious, my Marxism has struck deep roots and is purified. I believe armed fighting is the only solution for peoples struggling to free themselves, and I stick by my beliefs. Many will call me an adventurer, and I am one; but with a difference. One of those who risk their hides to prove their truths. Perhaps this time will be the last. I'm not looking for it, but it's within the logical realm of possibilities. If that's how it has to be, here's a last embrace.

I have loved you very much, but I haven't known how to express my affection. I'm extremely stiff in my behavior and I believe there were times when you didn't understand me. But, believe me now, understanding me wasn't easy.

Now, a will I've polished with an artist's care will hold up my flaccid legs and my exhausted lungs. I'll carry on.

Remember, once in a while, this small *condotieri [sic]* of the XX century. A kiss for Celia, Roberto, Ana Maria and Pototin, Beatriz, and everyone. A big embrace from your prodigal and recalcitrant son.

ERNESTO

To my children:
Dear Hildita, Aleidita, Camilo, Celia and Ernesto:

If you ever have to read this letter, it will be because I won't be with you.

You practically won't remember me, and the smaller ones won't remember at all.

Your father has been a man who acts as he believes and truly, he has been loyal to his convictions.

Grow up like good revolutionaries. Study hard so that you can master the technical ability to master nature. Remember that the revolution is the important thing and that each of us, alone, is worth nothing.

Above all, always be able to feel deeply any injustice committed against anyone in any part of the world. It's a revolutionary's most beautiful quality.

Until always, my children, I still hope to see you. A great big kiss and a hug from

PAPA

Ché's departure for Africa was a maneuver carefully planned by the Cuban political security service, run by Major Manuel Piñeiro, popularly known as "Redbeard." In July 1965, when Guevara was getting ready to travel to Cairo, the Cubans found a way to introduce a "secret report" into the office of the president of the military junta in the Dominican Republic, General Antonio Imbert Barrera. According to this "report," Ché had arrived in Santo Domingo the same day the military action began in April of that year, signing in at the Ambassador Hotel under the name of Oscar Ortiz. Later, he had moved to the Hotel Comercial, in Colonel Francisco Caamaño's sector, and had been killed during those wild days in a street skirmish. Although this version would not hold up under the slightest scrutiny since no guest with that name had checked into any of the hotels mentioned, General Imbert spent several weeks convinced that Ché had died in his country. Thus the whole world was thrown off the scent.

At that very moment Guevara was completing his preparations to leave for the Congo.

There, the armed contingents of Mulele and Soumialot were fighting Moise Tshombe's white mercenaries, a force that comprised a mixture of various nationalities, including a well-trained band of anti-Castro Cuban aviators.

Shortly before this Soumialot had said:

"We have no conditions to set for the cessation of our fighting, because it is our revolutionary struggle. And this struggle will never stop, in spite of the American bombers, tanks, and napalm bombs."

Guevara arrived in Brazzaville, where he found President Massemba-Debat, who had received him officially at the beginning of the year. There were a number of Cubans helping to organize European and American troops known as "mercenaries." In the following weeks, other Cubans joined the group, but their number never reached the thousands fancifully described by some reporters. At the point of greatest Cuban involvement, their men added up to fewer than two hundred, most of them instructors of para-military battalions.

The half-way position adopted by Cuba in the Sino-Soviet

dispute, at least in the interpretation of revolutionary methods, seems to account for Ché's presence in the Congo. In 1965 the Cubans began to develop the theory that they stood with the Soviet Union regarding international relations, and with China in their attitude toward popular fighting. This middle way proved very difficult to follow, and actually ended up as a dangerous game of skill. Cuba's spectacular position within the socialist world put a lot of pressure on the Russians, but Russia could return much more intense pressure through the silent tactic of economic support.

Ché stayed a little less than nine months in the Congo. He took part in several battles, particularly when the fighting was against well-equipped white mercenaries. Yet he was deeply upset by a tribal ritual in which the conqueror devoured the heart of his dead enemy at the end of the battle. This was supposed to enable the winner to transfer the mettle of the dead warrior to his own spirit and thereby increase his ability to fight. To men like Guevara, from advanced societies, the spectacle was repulsive.

In February 1966 Guevara sent a letter from Brazzaville to his oldest daughter, Hilda, on the occasion of her tenth birthday.

February 15

Dear Hildita:

I'm writing to you today, although the letter will not reach you 'til much later; but I want you to know I remember you and hope you're having a very happy birthday. You're almost a woman now and I can't write to you the way children are written to, telling them silly things and little white lies.

You must know that I'm far away and will still be far from you for a long time, doing all I can do to fight our enemies. Not that it's anything really big, but I'm doing something, and I think you'll always be able to be as proud of your father as I am of you.

Remember that you still have many years of struggle left and, even when you're a woman, you'll have to do your part. Meanwhile, you must prepare yourself, be very revolutionary, which at your age means that you must learn a lot, as much as possible, and always be ready to support just causes. You must also obey your mother and not imagine yourself ready for anything, ahead of time. That will come.

You must try hard to be one of the best in school. The best in every sense; you know what that means: studies and revolutionary activity, of course, good conduct, seriousness, love for the revolution, camaraderie, etc.

I wasn't like that at your age, but I was in a different society, where man was man's enemy. Now you have the privilege of living in a new epoch and you must be worthy of it.

Don't forget to keep your eyes open around the house and to look after the other kids and advise them to study and behave well, especially Aleidita, who respects you a lot as her older sister.

Well, *vieja*, once again, have a very happy birthday. Embrace your mother and Gina for me and receive for yourself a great big strong hug to last as long as we won't see each other from your

PAPA

Although on February 15, 1966, Guevara thought that he would remain in the Congo "a long time," his stay there would be over in another month. The end of Guevara's mission in Brazzaville was undoubtedly a result of the tension between Moscow and Peking and a reflection of this tension among the guerrilla commandos in the Congo. The policy of mediation between the USSR and China had a spectacular moment during the Havana Conference, better known as the Tricontinental Conference, held in January 1966. The Soviets tried to get closer, at least in theory, to the Chinese position on armed conflict. But Fidel Castro made a point of contrasting two kinds of support for revolutionary movements—"verbal" and "concrete." This was interpreted by the hundreds of delegates present as a backing of the Russians and a reproach to the Chinese.

The Chinese left Havana with serious misgivings about the Cuban position, for the Castro delegation had included the concept of peaceful coexistence in the wording of the final declaration, which was approved by a majority of votes, against the minority of Peking's allies. This coolness increased during the first week in February, when Castro publicly denounced the existence of a Chinese conspiracy to subvert the Cuban army, an allusion to Chinese distribution of anti-Soviet propaganda among the troops of the army. The Chinese thereupon stopped a shipment of rice they had promised Cuba.

This crisis in the relations between Peking and Havana had an immediate effect on Guevara's stay in the Congo. It is difficult to establish the sequence of events, since virtually no one in a position to shed light on the affair has done so. According to one version, the Chinese pressured the Cubans to leave. A different opinion holds that it was the Russians who asked Castro to withdraw his military delegation from the Congo. Finally, there is still another explanation that includes both these theories, according to which Soumialot, living in Cairo at the time, informed Castro that he must order Guevara to leave Brazzaville immediately, otherwise he would publicly denounce his presence there, setting off an international scandal.

At first Guevara refused to leave Africa. The emissary who brought him Castro's message was the same one who had taken the letter to Ché's daughter.

But Soumialot applied more pressure, and at the end of February two men who had Fidel Castro's full confidence and were also close friends of Ché's traveled to Cairo and from there to Brazzaville: Major Emilio Aragonés, a figure of the first rank in the Cuban hierarchy, and Major Drake, an officer of the army.

Aragonés and Drake explained the situation and stressed the need to obey Havana's orders at once without arguing. Again Cuba's fate was at stake. In March 1966 Guevara and his closest collaborators in the guerrilla war left the Congo, after a stay of almost nine months. They left as secretly as they had arrived.

9

Passion and Death in Bolivia

Bolivia's nationalist revolution, whose birth Guevara and I had witnessed in 1953, was dying at the end of 1964. Beset by difficulties, surrounded by countries generally hostile to its experiments in agrarian reform and its nationalization of mines, successive governments followed tradition, tolerating both the threats of political enemies and the discontent of proletarian friends. Geographical isolation, the price drop in the world market of its only export, tin, and the uncontrollable devaluation of the currency, combined to drag the reformist regime to disaster.

During that year, which marked the end of the nationalist government, a remarkable political phenomenon occurred that has yet to be clearly seen. In May, contingents of well-armed guerrillas appeared in the province of Santa Cruz, the eastern region touching Brazil's border. The guerrillas attacked army and frontier posts, set fire to sugar cane plantations, and moved about with extraordinary agility in an area overrun by wild vegetation. They bore a resemblance to a guerrilla force in the Castrista manner, whose tactics they copied, but the actual membership of this Bolivian insurgent band consisted of landowners and adherents of a small, active fascist party, the Bolivian *Falange*. Its organizer was a landowner of German extraction. He had assembled about eighty men on his property, and with them he had launched his operations. Naturally, the primary effect of these activities was political. Bolivian and foreign newspapers took them up and offered them as proof of the unrest prevailing in the country. The army, on its part, refrained from confronting the dissidents, although it had detachments of specialists in this type of warfare, trained by the United States military mission. These Rangers had been trained to fight not against guerrillas in general, but specifically against revolutionaries. Thus a "guerrilla" out to get rid of agrarian reform did not need to fear the Rangers.

The guerrillas in the countryside and the opposition in the cities both acted with an eye to one group: the officers of the army's extreme Right wing. The day the pincers' jaws were pressed together, the nationalist government fell, and a strong military regime took over. It was on November 4, 1964, less than six months after the strange fascist guerrillas had first appeared.

On the following day, the guerrillas dropped their mask, and, transformed into haughty landowners once more, they tried to take over the lands that had belonged to their fathers and grandfathers. At this point, the tough military government cracked down on its opposition. Deportation, exile into the jungle, the mobilization of striking workers became their new weapons of power. Yet this habitually brutal administration was very cautious concerning the laws governing property. The fascist ex-guerrillas were discouraged in several ways, the reformist laws stayed in force, and the Bolivian peasantry kept calm. Through a skillful and persistent demagogy the peasants came to feel themselves protected by the military government, and as a result they were ready to take up arms against the miners, the vanguard of the opposition.

From November 1964 the military government did nothing but expand its bases of support among the peasants. President René Barrientos, a dynamic air force general, had been born in an obscure village where he learned to speak the two Indian languages of the country, Aymará and Quechua. With this means of communication and a persuasive approach, including the distribution of elementary farming machinery, by 1966 Barrientos was able to say without boasting that his power rested not only on the army but also on the peasants.

In March of that year Guevara quietly came back to Cuba. He returned with his health worsened and a bitter "triumph" which he could not make public. Ché was sure his departure from the Congo had been a Russian maneuver, and that Moscow had come to an agreement with Washington on the general lines of African policy. In these, of course, there was no room for Guevara, and the Russians had passed the word on to Fidel Castro. Thus Guevara's worst suspicions, those he had discussed at length with Castro at the end of his tour in March 1965, had found new confirmation.

Ché now decided to return to his old dream of stirring up the peoples of the southern part of Latin America, of setting up a base in Bolivia, in northern Argentina, or in the south of Peru.

The operation was essentially the same as the one Masetti had turned into failure in 1964. Guevara studied reports on Argentina, Peru, and Bolivia. The government of the peaceful middle-roader, Doctor Arturo Illia, was still in power in Buenos Aires, and although there were signs of trouble, the climate there did not seem right for a repetition of Masetti's experiment. In Peru, a non-dictatorial, balanced civilian government had become especially proficient in repressing guerrillas. The most important rebel leaders were either dead or in prison.

But there was still Bolivia. The military government might come apart at any moment, and there was unrest in the mines.

This, in essence, was the report passed on to Havana by various young agitators of small leftist groups, all deadly enemies of the Bolivian Communist Party. The Communist Party itself accepted many points in this evaluation. Guevara concluded that if the Party agreed with the report in general but rejected violent action, it was one more proof of the Party's dependence on instructions from Moscow.

What no one apparently stressed was the peasants' support of the military government, although it is difficult to believe that it was not mentioned, since the new guerrillas were being recruited only from the rebel miners' organizations and the unemployed workers in the cities. (In this case, an analysis of the physical conditions seemed beside the point, since the miners, born on the high plateau or in the valleys, would have insurmountable difficulties when they came down to the tropical region.)

In his mistaken strategy, Guevara had a historical precedent in Lenin's fatal error, when he sent the Red Army to fight in Poland in 1920. Lenin also had incomplete and optimistic reports to go on, he was misled by the predictions of Polish Communist exiles living in Moscow, and he forgot that the Poles, whom he wanted to help liberate themselves, had strong nationalist tendencies. Lenin mobilized hundreds of agitators against Pilsudski. He convinced himself that the Polish peasants and workers would join the Red Army, and he kept the Second International Communist Congress in permanent session in the belief that he would be able to announce, from one day to the next, the establishment of a Communist government in Warsaw. Nevertheless, the Poles smashed the offensive of two unquestionable military talents—Tujachevski and Budienni—and the Russians had to fall back on Minsk in disorderly fashion just when they believed they had Warsaw in their grasp.

There were a number of important differences, but essentially Lenin's adventure in Poland was very similar to Guevara's in

Bolivia. For the most part both operations revealed that not only had the political situation been inconclusively analyzed, but the military preparation also suffered from serious defects.

Ché and Fidel were in complete accord about the organization of the guerrilla war in Bolivia. Castro believed the liberation movements on the continent had to be stepped up, mainly because Soviet appeasement policy, against all expectations, was actually smothering national guerrilla actions, beginning with Venezuela's, the most powerful of all.

The close link between Cuba's political and economic independence and the Latin American liberation movement was once more apparent; if the latter languished, the former would disappear. This interrelation undoubtedly encouraged the Cubans toward total commitment in the very center of South America.

There was at least one plenary session at which Guevara and all the members of the secret expedition discussed their plans with Castro.

"If you adapt yourself to the environment, you'll triumph," Castro told them. He knew the difficult conditions they would have to face.

Lenin had taken his chances on his Polish adventure so that at last capitalist Germany would have a socialist neighbor. He was obsessed with the idea of extending Russia's borders to the center of Europe. Guevara and Castro also wanted a Latin American border for Cuba, a socialist frontier closer than the Urals.

The core of Ché's guerrilla force was made up of sixteen men, most of them veterans of the famous Ciro Redondo column which Guevara had led during the war against Batista. It had fought the decisive battle of Santa Clara in 1958. There was no question that these men would follow him to hell, if that's where he wanted to go.

To get to Bolivia the contingent was split up into four groups.

Each man carried false identity documents issued, in two cases, by the authorities in Uruguay; in seven, by those of Panama; in seven others, by Ecuador's; and in two, by Colombia's. The discrepancy between the number of persons and the number of passports is explained by the fact that some of the men carried more than one document, keeping an extra one in case of emergency.

At least six of the contingent boasted the rank of major in the Cuban army, and several held important political jobs. Juan Vitalio Acuña Nuñez, for example, was a member of the Central Committee of the Cuban Communist Party and had been one of the first peasants to join Castro in the revolutionary war. Orlando Pantoja Tamayo had worked as assistant to Major Ramiro Valdés when he ran the G-2, the political police, before occupying the post of Minister of the Interior. Eliseo Reyes Rodríguez was one of the authentic heroes of the Cuban war, which he had joined at the age of sixteen. He had been promoted to captain during the famous march from Sierra Maestra to Las Villas. Reyes Rodríguez, called "San Luis" because he was born in the town of that name, was also in the Central Committee of the island's Communist Party. Another major was Gustavo Machín, onetime Vice-Minister in the Department of Industries. Jesús Cayol and Major Alberto Sánchez, who at one time ran Cuba's Bureau of Mines under Ché's supervision, belonged to the administrative apparatus.

Others were primarily "men of action," such as Daniel Alarcón Ramírez, who was the machine gunner in Camilo Cienfuegos' column when he was barely eighteen years old, or Harry Villegas Tamayo, who at twenty had been Ché's bodyguard. Some were leaving large families and solid official positions behind them. One of these was Leonardo Tamayo Núñez, a father of seven small children, who in 1961 was part of the Cuban staff at the economic conference of Punta del Este.

Major Pantoja Tamayo and two other men arrived in Bolivia from Peru, where Pantoja had been in 1963 when Hugo Blanco's peasant guerrillas were active in the valley of Cuzco. On that occasion his mission had been to find out at first hand the real strength of the guerrilla forces, ideologically rejected by the Peruvian Communists who were probably correct in ascribing a Trotskyist bias to Blanco. Pantoja's later mission had been to investigate how much was left of these Peruvian peasant forces and what collaboration could be expected from the survivors. At the end of August 1966, Pantoja and three companions arrived in Cochabamba, using regular means of transportation.

Ché, together with another man, entered Bolivia during the second week of September. He had left Havana on one of the regular flights of the Spanish airline, Iberia, stopping in Madrid and then continuing to Sao Paulo, Brazil. He had gone by bus to Corumbá, crossed over to Puerto Suárez, in Bolivian territory, and had immediately headed for the city of Cochabamba.

There, in the "garden city," the second most important in the country and the heart of its richest agricultural area, he had an interview a few days later with Jorge Kolle Cueto, a member of the Secretariat of the Bolivian Communist Party. Kolle's main purpose was to assure himself that Ché was in Bolivia; he supplied Ché with a general picture of the situation, with particular emphasis on military matters, which he knew well since his brother was a colonel and member of the army's top command. Although Ché insisted on some concrete form of collaboration, Kolle could not promise anything; the question could be decided only by the Party's Central Committee. But the answer would not be long in coming, he said. When the interview ended Kolle was still quite shaken: he would not have believed Ché was in Bolivia if he hadn't seen him with his own eyes.

In October five other men entered Bolivia from Arica, Chile. They had crossed the salt marsh of Uyuni, undergone a lurching ride on the cogwheel railway that grapples up the mountain slopes, and suffered the extreme distress of climbing almost ten thousand feet from the lowlands only to plunge back down to the valleys.

The last guerrillas finally arrived in December. Their trip had been long, from Havana to Leningrad, from Moscow to Prague, and then on to Buenos Aires. A doctor, Carlos Luna Martínez, called "Mogambo" by his companions, was in charge of the group. They too began learning immediately the hard life at this altitude, and when they reached La Paz, one of them passed out in the middle of the street.

Meanwhile, a network of Bolivians was laying the groundwork for guerrilla action. Between June and December 1966 a young Communist, Roberto Peredo, twenty-eight years old, covered the area around the town of Camiri in a jeep. One of the biggest oil camps in the country was located there. Peredo had been a cab driver, but he was also an experienced organizer. He had traveled several times to Cuba and had contributed to the plans now about to materialize. In Camiri, Choreti, Lagunillas, El Pincal, and Ñancahuazú he talked to persons he had known or to whom he had letters of introduction. He explained that he wanted to buy a farm and devote himself to cattle raising; he finally found a large piece of property in Ñanchahuazú, where he started to run a cattle farm and grow agricultural produce, especially peanuts. The farm had great possibilities for feeding a large number of people with its produce, but the guerrilla camp was set up far away in order not to arouse suspicion. The men would slip away during the night without drawing attention. Even so, the neighbors became suspicious, thinking that they were planting poppies in order to manufacture narcotics.

The farmhouse had a crenelated zinc roof, so that the rain water would run down. This kind of zinc was called "calamine" in the region. It was a generic name for these roofs, but in this area, where they were rarely found, it was used as a code name. The guerrilla conspiracy was being hatched in the "calamine house."

Peredo took his jeep every day to Camiri, the oil city, where commercial traffic was very busy. There he stocked up on food, clothing, and medicines, in proportion to the increase in the contingent's membership and its growing needs.

Other men were recruiting soldiers from the mines, where for some time an impotent resentment had been building up against the military government. The regime had fenced in the working zones with barbed wire, like concentration camps, and didn't miss a chance to jail and deport union leaders. The news spread quietly, in whispers, through the dark shafts and tunnels of the mines. A sense of danger began to run like an electric current through the miserable shanties, slipping into the men's quick conversations and showing in the eyes of the women.

The government was not supposed to get wind of what was going on. Nevertheless, it received reports, incomplete but sufficiently revealing to indicate that something important was brewing. Apparently the first news the administration received concerned a violent quarrel among the Communists in the mines, the reopening of a dispute that had been considered closed between followers of Peking and those of Moscow. The government suspected that it wasn't a question of theoretical differences any more, but rather something more concrete: the old controversy over revolution by peaceful or violent means had come up again because somebody, at that very moment, was proposing the latter for Bolivia.

The government took special precautions. In November it managed to establish that Guevara had actually entered Bolivia two months before and was now finishing a reconnaissance tour of the south, meeting with political leaders in the cities. There was considerable stir among all leftist circles, for Guevara didn't shy from discussion with any sector, whether it followed the

Chinese line or, even worse, maintained old loyalties to Trotsky's ideas.

A hard alternative faced the Bolivian Communist Party. It could not reject outright its analysis of the situation, beginning with the need for armed struggle. But if it chose the latter, it was clearly running counter to Soviet strategy, and if it didn't, Guevara would depend exclusively on the hated pro-Chinese and the more abysmal Trotskyites. The Central Committee wavered, not knowing which way to turn. Many of the orthodox Communists feared that in such a confusion of different tendencies split by old conflicts the Party would end up having worked against Moscow's instructions and having lost the guerrilla movement as well.

In the begining of December 1966 Mario Monje, the Secretary General of the Bolivian Communist Party, traveled to Havana to discuss the matter with Castro. The Cuban leader found himself in an awkward position. He could not ignore the pacts between the Latin American Communist Parties and Moscow, and at the same time he had to obtain the support of the Bolivian Communists for his friend Guevara. What Castro was practically asking Monje was to let the political leadership on the continent be transferred from Moscow to Havana.

Monje returned with a clearer picture, and on New Year's Day, 1967, he asked to be taken to the camp at Ñancahuazú, where he had a long but not very friendly talk with Ché. Guevara had already noticed various signs of disaffection on the part of the Bolivian Communists. His agitators in the mines had been ignored, and in other cases men who had seemed ready to join the camp had changed their minds at the last minute.

"The Party can't commit itself officially in the guerrilla war," Monje told him, "but it can be done in another way, for instance, if I resign my post first. Then, I co ıld follow, with the guerrillas, a line parallel to the Party's, without being in the Party."

The idea didn't seem bad to Guevara. Besides, it had been tried before in other places. But Monje's demands grew.

"I ought to supervise negotiations with other groups," he added. "It would be a shame if adventurers and provocateurs infiltrated, don't you think?"

Guevara liked this idea less. He knew that Monje would keep out all pro-Chinese, Trotskyites, and those expelled from the Communist Party, and this attitude clashed with his wide concept of popular war.

Nevertheless, he continued listening intently to Monje's proposals.

"Finally," Monje said, "as long as operations are carried out on Bolivian territory, I'll be the military and political leader."

"Certainly not," Guevara answered. "I am the leader."

It had been a rough discussion, and Ché's final words would always ring in the Communist leader's ears:

"My failure would not mean that the fight can't be won. Many failed trying to climb Everest, but Everest was finally conquered."

The following dawn, Guevara managed to hear a broadcast of a speech by Fidel Castro from Havana. Castro knew nothing about Ché's negotiations with Monje, but speaking to the crowd gathered to celebrate the eighth anniversary of the triumph of the revolution, he exclaimed:

"And our message is special and warm because it comes from deep inside us, from the affection born in the heat of our struggles; our message, in whatever part of the world he may be, to Major Ernesto Guevara and his companions."

A profound silence fell on the camp at Ñancahuazú.

Then came more for them.

"The imperialists have killed Ché many times in many places, but we hope that someday, when imperialism least expects it,

Major Ernesto Guevara will be born from his ashes, like the phoenix, a fighting, healthy guerrilla, and that we'll once more have actual news from Ché."

That night the guerrillas went to sleep filled with hope. They weren't alone. They would win.

Volunteers began arriving. They had been recruited in the tin mines, and each group came with its leaders. Moisés Guevara was the union leader of the San José mine, in the district of Oruro. He was thirty, had four small children, and was a mechanic. On January 19, 1967, Guevara reached the guerrilla camp, where he introduced himself to the other Guevara, Ché.

A month later eight other men, also comrades of Guevara the miner, joined the band. Among them came Simón Cuba, who would play an important role in events to come.

Negotiations continued in Havana. Two leaders of the Bolivian Communist Party traveled to Cuba, Jorge Kolle, who had met with Ché, and Simón Reyes.

Reyes was a thirty-five-year-old miner, Secretary of Relations for the Union of Mine Workers. He was in the thick of the agitation in the mines, but had refused to join the guerrillas because he feared one possible consequence: he was sure the government would attribute foreign control to the miners' struggle when it discovered Ché was the head of the guerrillas. In this event, Reyes said, the harm would be far greater than the benefit. The two Bolivians held the last official negotiation with Castro concerning the attitude of the Communist Party toward the guerrilla war. They both stressed the same problem: the force at Ñancahuazú was a magnet drawing all the heterodox elements of the Bolivian Left and had assumed a form dangerous to official Communism. Although it was never openly admitted, it became clear that Guevara could not count on the Communist Party organization, its supply and communication lines, or its member groups. Both Castro and Guevara held a bad opinion of the Bolivian Communist Party, but for all its lack of fight and its sad proletarian cadres, it had assumed great importance if the isolation of the guerrilla forces was to be avoided.

The zone of operations remained quiet. Were one to examine a map of the province of Santa Cruz, this wouldn't seem strange. The map shows a completely uninhabited quadrangle, bounded on the west by the cities of Camiri and Santa Cruz, in the east by Puerto Suárez, and to the north by Concepción and San Ignacio. The absence of any sign of habitation in the center of the area is not an omission of the cartographers. The population is almost nonexistent over the entire region. This becomes clear if we compare this one province in Bolivia with other countries. Its surface is equal to that of Great Britain, Belgium, and Cuba combined, yet it has only 340,000 inhabitants, its population density averaging about three people per square mile.

The ranch of Ñancahuazú was located in the middle of this vast wild desert. The main road of the province passed through an insignificant village, Lagunillas, where six hundred people lived, although the locals regarded it as a city. A dirt road started at Lagunillas and ended at El Pincal ranch. It could be covered by jeep in less than an hour. From then on, there were several trails difficult to travel on, and the terrain turned rough. There were deep passes. The forest was dense, its vegetation packed tight. Creepers made the entire region impenetrable, so much so that it was possible to make out a man or a crouching animal six feet ahead of you. A precipice hedged the Ñancahuazú River, which crossed the farm where Ché had his general headquarters. The river had a narrow beach, interrupted at intervals, forcing a cut-back into the jungle that struggled up the escarpments. There were clouds of voracious mosquitoes, called *mariguies* by the local people. But the worst enemy of the civilian soldier or guerrilla fighter, the peasant or the explorer, was the thick, unyielding, thorny vegetation. The thickets were overrun by lianas and other vines, and spiny plants of the cactus family with huge, serrated leaves. Flesh and clothing were left on these plants, ripped off in strips.

Accidents were regular in this hostile terrain. On February 26th a Bolivian miner and member of the guerrilla forces slipped over the edge of a ravine and was killed. Soon others would die, drowned in the river's wild rapids or their bodies crushed when they lost their footing high up and plummeted onto the rocks below.

Camp life was arduous, but there was always work to do while waiting for the fighting to start. One group took up the systematic study of Quechua, the language of the local Indians, also spoken by many peasants. They did assignments in notebooks and learned to conjugate verbs and construct complete sentences. In this way they hoped to get much closer to the local peasants.

By February the men had consumed all their food supplies. New Year's Eve, when they listened to Fidel Castro speaking from Havana, had passed into their store of pleasant memories. That night they had had suckling pig, nougat from Spain, beer and cider.

Not a sound had been heard from their comptroller, who lived in La Paz. Shortly afterward Guevara would find out that this comptroller, who had been picked for his great trustworthiness, had simply double-crossed them, skipping out at the worst moment with a quarter of a million dollars which he had received to buy supplies and ship them to Ñancahuazú.

The guerrillas hunted. They trapped monkeys and wild pigeons and ate them roasted, joking about it. There were deserters. Some weapons and an anesthetizer were lost.

Near the end of February a group of five men, at least two of them Cubans, made brief contact with the peasants. They were received with suspicion. They looked like foreigners and history had taught the peasants always to expect the worst from outsiders. They directed them to the Río Grande and, as soon as the men had left, notified the army.

The guerrillas were seen later by other peasants. They had just waded across the Río Grande and one of them had let some Bolivian and dollar bills get wet. He took them out of a wide money belt with big pockets, one by one, and patiently spread them out to dry in the sun. The small contingent was carrying out a reconnaissance mission, without supplies, and more than once, they had fed on dead fish they found in the backwater of some river. Their march had been slow, often covering barely one mile a day.

The army, already warned that persons in military uniform, most of them bearded, were prowling in the region north of Camiri, sent out scouting parties, but the task was as difficult for the soldiers as it was for the guerrillas, and aerial photography failed miserably, since ground visibility was less than 20 per cent.

On March 16th, two miners in Moisés Guevara's group deserted, exhausted by privations and disillusioned by the lack of real fighting. Three days later an army patrol discovered a cache which threw a good deal of light on what was going on. The deserters had left a trail. Civilian clothing for no fewer than ten men was found in six large suitcases and several smaller ones. Some suits had labels embroidered "Casa Albion, de Habana."

This find had singular importance for the army. They assumed there were, in fact, a large number of Cubans in the Bolivian jungle. Why shouldn't Ché Guevara himself be among them? The entire security network of the hemisphere was shaken by the news, and Colonel Kolle, Commander in Chief of the Air Force and brother of the Communist leader, left for Buenos Aires and Rio de Janeiro to seek aid appropriate to the importance of the persons operating in his country.

The army prepared for war and began random patroling of the region. One of these patrols surprised, and in turn was surprised by, a guerrilla advance party they ran into, almost head on, captained by the Cuban major Antonio Díaz. Díaz had no orders to engage in battle, and to avoid it he chose the dangerous tactic of falling back on general headquarters at Ñancahuazú. All the army had to do now to find them was simply to follow his tracks. Only a question of time.

Ché heard Díaz's explanation angrily. They argued and Ché finally stripped him down to private.

He also decided to engage in battle immediately, the sooner the better now that they had been found out.

The guerrillas' biggest victory took place on March 23rd. The army force was left with seven dead and four wounded, and nine had been taken prisoner. Six Mauser rifles, three machine guns, and a considerable amount of ammunition were captured by the insurgents.

As a result of this clash a new situation arose in the complex intrigue of political support for the guerrillas. The prisoners they had taken were returned the next day, blindfolded, and the wounded among them given first-aid treatment. There were two officers, who were freed without their uniforms or their weapons. Deeply humiliated, they gave a blown-up account of the guerrilla forces that had surprised them, in order to save face. On the basis of their declaration the army believed for a long time that the guerrillas numbered more than five hundred.

The battle had certainly proved that the rebels were an efficient and well-armed contingent. The officers' statements were accepted as gospel truth, first by the army, which had to cover up its defeat, and immediately afterward by the Central Committee for the Communist Party. The latter called an emergency meeting and on the last day of March issued a statement of solidarity with the guerrilla movement. Strangely enough, it bore the signatures of Monje and Kolle Cueto, who had been unable to get together with either Ché or Fidel Castro about the conditions under which they would provide support. Despite this sudden show of fight, however, no effective collaboration left the cities for the farm at Ñancahuazú.

The day after the clash, the Air Force strafed the guerrilla sector. The army began a vast encircling operation, concentrating two thousand soldiers in the area, and helicopters and the American Green Berets were put into action. CIA agents also arrived on the spot. The La Paz radio stations were sure that there were more than seven hundred guerrillas.

A mood of unrest now hovered over the guerrilla camp. Food supplies had steadily dwindled, and there was a virtual cessation of news from the outside, with the exception of radio broadcasts, mostly Bolivian and therefore not very reliable. Ché began to feel the important need for a "frontier of support"; during the People's War in China this had been the Russian frontier, in Viet Nam's case it had been the frontier of China, and in Cuba's it had been the United States and Costa Rica. In Bolivia, on the other hand, the frontier countries unanimously backed the government against the guerrillas. The armies of Argentina, Brazil, and Peru formed a solid line along their borders with Bolivia. It was inconceivable that any material help—even an airplane loaded with arms, like the ones that aided Castro in Sierra Maestra—could break through this tight military ring.

Ché realized that the situation could not swing in his favor unless a fundamental change took place in the political climate of the cities. This was a job that required the help of a political organization, and Guevara had none. For some days after the Communist Party announced its adherence to the guerrillas' cause, Guevara waited for new Communist emissaries to arrive. But it quickly became clear to him that the Communist Party's support would go no farther than the announcement, and that fundamentally its opposition to his forces remained unchanged.

He could have sought the collaboration of the majority party, the MNR, but he didn't trust its leaders and they, in turn, didn't want to be implicated in a Communist uprising. They still had many important ties with the military and with certain powerful factions in the United States. All this would have been lost if the MNR accepted Ché as military leader.

The military blockade, then, reinforced the political blockade. No doubt Guevara's cause was hurt by his inflexibility, which did not permit him to seek an alliance with the opposition parties as Fidel Castro had done in 1958. In subscribing to the Pact of Caracas Castro had completely misrepresented the radical intentions of his movement, making them passable and even deserving of praise from the political professionals. This maneuver later allowed him to bargain with Batista's own ranking officers, softened up by the politicos whose fears, in turn, had been quieted by the signing of the pact. Guevara had told me on more than one occasion that Castro's political talent was extraordinary, and now he had fresh proof of it in contrast to his own situation. Undoubtedly, Castro would not have been trapped in such a difficult position. He would have been willing to try anything, no matter how contradictory it looked at the time, in order to rescue his men from political isolation and military impotence. In a situation like this Castro would no doubt have been willing to turn over the leadership to Monje, the Communist, if, in exchange, the whole machinery of the Communist Party were thrown into the conflict. Guevara, however, was not willing to do this.

The Bolivian president, General Barrientos, momentarily rejected the idea that Ché could be in his country, despite the insistence of some of his military chiefs. The radio stations broadcast the general's assurances: "The man is dead, like his friend Camilo Cienfuegos."

But the Commander in Chief of the army persisted in his suspicion. "The guerrillas don't want to abandon their present zone," he said, "because they have important persons there, perhaps foreign leaders whom they have to protect." And just in case he was right, he reinforced the troops to three thousand men.

Early in April Ché received another setback. Ex-President Paz Estenssoro, who had been ousted by the military and lived in exile in Lima, declared that the guerrillas were Communists and that, accordingly, the people would not back them, because the predominant sentiment of the country was nationalist. Thus, Guevara's refusal to talk things over with Bolivia's most important popular party increased his political isolation even more. The country's principal political groups belonged to either the Communist Party or the MNR, and now they had both left the guerrilla band to fend for itself.

On April 10th the rebel column clashed with the army once more, very close to Ñancahuazú, at a place called Iripití. Eleven soldiers died in the skirmish, seven were wounded, and eleven were taken prisoner, among them an officer. The guerrillas also had casualties, but they got a valuable recompense. They captured thirty-five weapons, some of them brand new.

After this skirmish Ché decided to let two friends who had joined him on special conditions leave camp. One was the French professor Régis Debray, a very close friend of Castro's. He had come to Bolivia from Havana by an indirect flight. His presence there had publicity value more than anything else, for it was hoped that via the European newspapers, he would make known the existence of the Bolivian guerrilla forces and, when the right time came, the spectacular news that Guevara was their leader. Debray had been in Ñancahuazú since March 6th. He had arrived with another man, Ciro Bustos, an Argentine. The latter had been summoned to "an important political meeting," which Ché could attend; what he had not been told was that this "meeting" was really the outbreak of the guerrilla war. He shared Guevara's ideas, in general, but in this case he disagreed about the way things had been prepared and about the timing. He let Ché know this, but since he respected and admired him, he didn't find it easy. Still, he maintained his criticism of the project. Guevara ended up admitting that two of his objections, the lack of information about the surrounding countryside and the shortage of regular supplies, were valid.

The narrow canyon of the Ñancahuazú River was surrounded by the army, and Guevara didn't know just how to get Debray and Bustos through the encirclement. He finally let them leave in a direction that seemed safe. It wasn't. On April 20th an army patrol stopped them as they walked through the small town of Muyupampa.

Ché regretted his imprudence. His two most direct couriers to the outside world—perhaps the only two for a very long time, the way things were going—were now in the hands of the army.

A short time before he had managed to send to Havana a "Message to the Peoples of the World," made public on April 16th by the Organization of Solidarity of the Peoples of Africa, Asia and Latin America. Six photographs of Ché, two in civilian clothing and four in uniform, probably taken in the jungle, although there was no mention where, were delivered with this declaration. This was the famous recommendation to the revolutionaries of the world to take up arms and "create two, three, many Vietnams"—a tragic analysis of the international political situation, in which he questioned every basis on which world peace dangerously rested.

"The solidarity of the progressive world with the people of Vietnam," he wrote, "resembles the bitter irony that the cheers of the plebians signified for the gladiators in the Roman circus. It should not be a matter of wishing the victim success, but of sharing his very fate, accompanying him to death or victory."

This had a violent anti-Soviet implication, although it didn't mention the USSR, and in a way it was also an attack on the Chinese. Ché confessed his "anguish" before the "isolation of the Vietnamese."

He was probably thinking of his own isolation.

The clashes now became more frequent as the army's "mopping

up," a yard-by-yard operation, began to shrink the area in which the guerrilla band could move.

At El Mesón, a place south of Monte Dorado, on the outer slopes of the Ñancahuazú range, the guerrillas once again surprised an army patrol, inflicting two casualties. They also killed a police dog, trained for jungle fighting by the Americans.

Two weeks later the guerrillas struck suddenly in Taparilla, killing two more men; almost immediately afterward they attacked again, killing three army men, one of them an officer, and wounding several others.

It was at this time that Guevara and Roberto Peredo, the Bolivian leader, took time out to draw up a document, the guerrillas' first manifesto, announcing the creation of the National Liberation Army of Bolivia. Its text, presumably written in the middle of May, although it was dated in April, is as follows:

THE NATIONAL LIBERATION ARMY OF THE BOLIVIAN PEOPLE.

The story of privations and sufferings our people have endured and are still enduring is a long one. For hundreds of years rivers of blood have been flowing uninterruptedly. The mothers, wives, children, and sisters who have shed floods of tears run into the thousands. The lives of thousands of heroic patriots have been cut down.

We men of this country have lived like foreigners. Any Yankee imperialist has more rights, which he calls his "concessions," in our homeland. He can raze or burn down houses, destroy arable lands, any property of Bolivians. Our lands aren't ours, our natural resources have served and are still serving to make foreigners rich, leaving us Bolivians only terrible wounds in our lungs. There is no schooling for our children, there are no hospitals. The conditions of our lives are miserable. We are paid starvation wages and salaries. Thousands of men, women, and children die of hunger every year. The destitution in which the peasants live and work is terrifying. In other words, we live under conditions of slavery with our rights and our earnings denied us, crushed underfoot.

In May 1965, before the shocked eyes of the whole world, salaries were cut, workers dismissed, locked up, exiled, massacred, and the oil camps, with defenseless women and children, bombed and looted.

Although this is the picture of how we live, ours was and is a fighting people that never let itself be brought to its knees.

How many heroes among the miners, peasants, factory hands, teachers, professional men, and our glorious youth, the students, have written with their blood the most glorious pages of our history! There before us and the world, we have, in places of honor, the legendary figures of Padilla, Lamza, Méndez, Sudanes, Nervelo, Murillo, Tupacamarú, Warners, Arze, and also our unparalleled heroines at La Coronilla, Juana Azurduy de Padilla, Bartolina Sisa, whose glorious examples our heroic people remember and are ready to follow.

Although former generations bore up under a bloody fifteen-year war to build a free, sovereign country, throwing the foreign master out of our land, before many years had passed new capitalist powers sank their claws into our country, built by Bolívar and Sucre. The peasants brutally assassinated from the founding of the Republic until today add up to thousands upon thousands; thousands are the miners and factory workers whose demands were answered with machine guns. Also in the thousands are the "brave" colonels who have won their promotions and rankings in this one-sided battle, machine gunning and bombing the defenseless people that, time and again, rises armed with nothing but that wall of courage which never bends or degrades itself.

The memory of massacres, crimes, and insults to which the Bolivian people have been submitted remains fresh in our minds. Overseers, generals, and Yankee imperialists, your claws and your jaws are red with the blood of the Bolivian people, and today your final hour has tolled, the final hour of the pools of blood you have spilled in abundance, of the ashes of thousands of patriots you have assassinated, persecuted, imprisoned and exiled. Today the National Liberation Army rises. Men from the fields and the cities, from the mines and the factories, from schools and universities, are bravely taking up arms.

Assassins, the voice of justice, well-being, and liberty also announces that your hour has come and it echoes over Bolivia, with a quiet sound that cannot be stopped, on the mountains and in the valleys, in the jungles and on the high plateau.

Generals, today when you receive your first blows, you will scream for your mothers and your children; we too are sorry for them. But, can you possibly believe that those thousands of peasants, laborers, teachers, and students did not also have children, mothers, and wives? Those you murdered mercilessly in the streets of the cities, in Catavi, Cerdas, Villa Victoria, El Alto, La Paz, Milluni, and Siglo XX?

Before the vigorous onset of our struggle, the ruling clique and its master, Yankee imperialism, tremble with fear. They paw the air like cornered beasts, persecution increases, they feel impelled to commit greater crimes, to violate their pseudo-democratic constitution, having sworn to respect it. Their anti-guerrilla hysteria leads them to outlaw political parties of the Left, as if they could kill ideas with a decree. They persecute, imprison, assassinate ("suicide") free citizens, accusing them of being guerrillas. They seize and torture foreign correspondents, trying to prove that they are guerrillas. They slander and weave their propaganda on the basis of lies so laughable that the people scorn them. This and every attempt they make to stifle the guerrilla movement will be in vain, and in vain all their attempts to try to stay in power. Their end as a ruling body is at hand.

We are sorry that in this struggle, which is necessary to wipe out robbery, abuse, injustice, crime, and the sinecures a few enjoy, to build a new classless society where social justice prevails with equal duties and rights for everyone, where natural resources may be exploited for the people and the benefit of the people, many lives will be lost that can be useful to the country, among the officers as well as soldiers, because surely not all who are sent to the battlefield think along the same lines as the pro-Yankee clique that holds power.

We call on all patriots, officers, and soldiers to put down their arms; on the country's glorious youth, not to join the army. On mothers, to stop their boys from being sacrificed to defend a clique that has sold out to the foreigner's dollar and hands over the best of our riches to voracious Yankee imperialism.

The National Liberation Army calls on the Bolivian people to close ranks, to weld the tightest unity without distinction of political colors; on those patriots who are capable of fighting, to join the ranks of the National Liberation Army. It is also possible to help from outside; there are a thousand ways of doing it, and the creative genius of the people will know how to find the various methods, from groups of friends to more daring ways. The problem is to organize and make the governing clique and its master, Yankee imperialism, feel the Bolivian ground tremble under their feet. We warn the people that, in order to keep our country in its grip, Yankee imperialism will turn to new generals and civilians, and even pseudo-revolutionaries, whom in turn it will drop when the time comes. We warn it not to let itself be surprised and deceived as has happened throughout our history. This time the fight has begun and will not end until the day the people governs itself and foreign dominion has been wiped out.

We warn that the National Liberation Army will take care to carry out the ideals of the people, will punish in due time the present oppressor, torturer, informer, and traitor, those who commit injustices against the poor that go unpunished. The organizations for civil defense are in the process of formation. Popular revolutionary courts will begin to take action, trying and sentencing.

Finally, the National Liberation Army expresses its faith, its confidence, and its conviction in the triumph over the Yankees, and the invaders disguised as advisors, Yankees or otherwise. We shall not let ourselves rest until we see the last stronghold of imperialist domination freed, until we see the happiness, progress, and good fortune of the Bolivian people shining forth.

Die rather than live as slaves!
Long live the guerrillas!
Death for Yankee imperialism and its military clique!
Liberty for all patriots under arrest and in prison!

NATIONAL LIBERATION ARMY
Ñancahuazú, April 1967

The manifesto had practically no circulation in Bolivia, except among small political groups. It was sent abroad and was reproduced in several countries, but it didn't change the feeling current among the most knowledgable observers: the guerrillas were in a trap; military forces, getting better at jungle fighting day by day, were at their heels.

A guerrilla column moved eastward to where the railway runs between Yacuiba, on the Argentine border, and Santa Cruz, in the north. There were skirmishes near El Espino and Muchiría, and the column turned northward. It crossed the Rió Grande, near Abapó, a sleepy town, and advanced up the left bank of the river to where it meets the Rositas River. Another skirmish took place there. Now following the Rositas River the column arrived at the Morocos River. At a place called Piraí, there was a new, violent clash with the army, in which three guerrillas died.

The column was made up of the best men Ché had at his disposal, including Cuban veterans. Its march northward was intended to take it to the highway joining the cities of Cochabamba and Santa Cruz. By going into the more populated areas the guerrillas hoped to break down their total isolation in the canyon of Ñancahuazú.

Reliable and sensible, Major Acuña Núñez, the leader of the column, would never expose his men unnecessarily, yet he was capable of conceiving the boldest operations. On this occasion he planned and executed a spectacular maneuver. On July 7th the guerrillas blocked off the road between Santa Cruz and Cochabamba, in a place called Las Cuevas. They cut the telephone lines and seized a passenger bus. With this vehicle, which was carrying a group of traveling students who now suddenly found themselves joining, enthusiastically, an adventure as extraordinary as any they would see in the movies, the guerrillas rode into the town of Samaipata. The occupation of this town lasted barely over an hour, but it stirred up a good deal of political dust. While some men arrested the local authorities, others got hold of clothing, food, and medicines. There was even time for a political harangue before the frightened eyes of the peasants.

I arrived in La Paz on July 12th, five days after this incident, to take over Ciro Bustos' legal defense. Obviously public opinion had been aroused. The guerrillas were cut off from the whole world, yet they had shown themselves capable of pulling off a feat of imagination and courage, right under the noses of the military, making them look like fools, taking over a town and supplying themselves at will with everything they needed. People found this story very exciting and, at the same time, far removed from their lives. They read about it in the papers, learned the most insignificant details, and embellished it with their own imaginations. It was certainly one of the worst moments for the government of Barrientos, who himself tried hard to keep calm.

I remained in La Paz for two weeks. The military authorities at first would not let me go on to Camiri, where Bustos and Debray were being held. They were dawdling between two alternatives: converting the town into the scene of a world spectacle for their travesty of justice, or holding the trial of Bustos and Debray behind closed doors. The second was apparently the choice of many important army chiefs, but in the end they were overruled by the belligerent demagoguery of General Barrientos and his agents among the secret police.

Actually, if the military tribunal had tried the prisoners in accordance with the law, the Bolivian constitution itself, reformed by the military, would have stopped them from condemning the two men. But the trial would then be meaningless and the political benefit Barrientos hoped to reap from it would vanish into thin air. It was a question of whipping up the simplest kind of patriotism, particularly in the peasant communities, stressing the point that the prisoners must logically belong to an expeditionary force made up of hundreds of foreigners, all of them intruders and enemies of the Bolivian people. From the capital the country was flooded with handbills signed by a mysterious committee of "The Ladies of Camiri," explaining in a simplistic way the "foreign invasion" and its dangers to the material and moral heritage of the Bolivians. There was even a hint that the peasants could be stripped of their lands by these revolutionaries who came from far away.

There's no question that the trial was a scandal, a juridical monstrosity. Once I realized that Barrientos had had his way, using the trial as a political instrument, nothing that happened later could surprise me. As I learned when I finally got to Camiri, Bustos had been kept incommunicado for sixty days, although the constitution dictated by the military specified a maximum of two days in such cases. Even worse, the Commander in Chief of the Bolivian Army himself had used his authority to make sure that no lawyer for the defense was assigned the case until three months after Bustos' arrest. Naturally, the prisoner was tortured by agents of the Bolivian secret service, whom the military bosses constantly pressed for information while the guerrillas tirelessly continued their operations.

The MNR was not taking part in the war, but like all the other parties it was ready to use it in order to topple the military government. Barrientos as well as his army colleagues were aware of this plan and tried to stop it. They had worked with sporadic success in the political field ever since their declaration during the first days in June that the country was in a state of siege. This had been followed by a series of arrests of party heads, mostly in the MNR, and an attempt by Barrientos to implicate the MNR leaders with the guerrilla forces. But the police measures irritated the people in the cities and drove many agitators into the mining camps.

During the months of June and July political instability throughout the country reached its peak. On June 24th the army attacked the miners of Catavi, who were demonstrating in the mining area, killing forty of them and wounding more than a hundred. And yet this massacre, which became known as the "Massacre of San Juan," did not work in favor of Ché's guerrillas. The latter's failure to communicate was clear now; the two sympathetic actions, the guerrillas' and the miners', failed to end in a common understanding. They remained parallel, each following alone its own road to extinction.

The holding of Samaipata had placed the government in a foolish light and thrown doubt on the efficacy of the army. Three days later, two of the three government parties withdrew their support. The regime tottered.

Whipped into action by an atmosphere that was growing more unfavorable every day, the army made an effort to take its revenge. On July 20th, it fought a battle on the banks of the Morocos River, where Ché and his men had set up camp.

It was the first clash provoked by the army and the first time Ché's camp was caught off guard. The soldiers captured material of inestimable value to the guerrillas, who were in no position to replace any losses: ten haversacks, radios, walkie-talkies, weapons and ammunition.

The army's offensive now became firmer and more systematic.

The professional influence of the Green Berets began to make itself felt. Among these American advisers were eleven superspecialists, brought to Bolivia from Vietnam to instruct six hundred and fifty Bolivian Rangers in an accelerated program. The native Rangers went through nineteen weeks of intensive training. The first seven days were dedicated to rifle and mortar practice, camouflage, identification of targets, and listening for movements at night. Then they went on to learn ambush and counterambush tactics, continuing their training until they were sent to the front. The soldiers were good students. Ché recognized their skill and stamina, but Major Shelton, the head of the Green Berets, preferred to put emphasis on the economic side.

"It costs $400,000 to kill a Viet Cong," he commented, "but in Bolivia it's much cheaper."

I saw how correctly Shelton had sized up the situation a short time later, when I attended a pathetic ceremony in which the Rangers, who had just fought a successful battle against the guerrillas, killing many of them, were given an award. It was in Santa Cruz, where I had gone to ask for a pass to continue as far as Camiri. The military commander of the region thought it fitting that I wait for him several hours. In the central courtyard of a rambling old house used as a barracks thirty-five soldiers stood in formation. Suddenly, they snapped to attention as the town notables, the board of directors of the local Rotary Club, arrived. They were carrying small packages, which they stacked on a table of unfinished wood. There was a speech lauding Western civilization, and a few minutes later a lady began handing out the packages. The soldiers opened them avidly, and I saw what was in each: a set of underwear and a tin of sardines. It was the salary for their fear, their reward for the cruel fight against the guerrillas. Obviously Major Shelton had not been exaggerating.

On August 31st the army set a trap for Major Acuña Núñez's

column of seventeen guerrillas. It was carefully laid, after a peasant boy warned a soldier that two guerrillas had entered his house looking for food while his father was fishing far away on the river.

The spot was called Vado del Yeso (Chalk Ford). Here the clean waters of the Masicuri River and the turbulent, sandy current of the Río Grande crossed. There was a beach on either side and, beyond the beaches, thick jungle.

The two guerrillas had promised to come back the next day. When the military heard this, they had the absent peasant's wife return home to receive the guerrillas as if nothing were wrong. Meanwhile, the army hid behind some bushes and sat down to wait patiently.

The peasant owner of the hut had come back by then and was quickly instructed on what to do. The main thing was to wear a white shirt so that the soldiers wouldn't mistake him and kill him too.

Major Acuña Núñez finally appeared. As he crossed the river, he scooped up some water in his hand and drank it. The others followed behind. He was on the beach and on his way to the forest when the shooting began. Acuña Núñez and a soldier exchanged bullets at short range and both fell dead at the same time. The others dropped their haversacks to move more freely in the river, and soon the waters were carrying objects difficult to make out. Some were haversacks, others men. From the beach, the soldiers fired at everything. The river turned red with blood. The column lost nine men. The remaining eight retreated, now poorly armed and leaderless.

Paco, a Bolivian, was taken prisoner by the army, and Captain Mario Vargas, in charge of the troop, ordered him to identify the dead bodies one by one.

"This is Joaquín [Acuña Núñez], the leader. This one, Braulio, the second in command. This one, Alejandro, chief of operations of the entire guerrilla force. This is Moisés Guevara." Paco was about to go on, but the officer broke in.

"Is he by any chance Ché's brother?" he asked, surprised.

"No," Paco continued, "he's a Bolivian mining leader. That one over there is Polo. The other's name is Walter, and the other is Maimura, our doctor."

"Is anybody missing?" the captain continued.

"Yes, Tania, who always brought up the rear. Looks as if the waters carried her off. And the other doctor, the Peruvian called Blackie."

Two days later, the fugitives fought with the army again at Yajo Pampa, in the same Rió Grande area, and lost four more men. Acuña Núñez's column, once thought so dangerous, was down to four.

In the meantime Ché kept on the move with his own men. He had only twenty at this point. He had a hard time trying to feed them and got no help from the peasants. In fact, not a single peasant had joined his forces.

Lenin's campaign in Poland inevitably comes to mind again. The words Lenin wrote to Clara Zetkin, explaining his failure, seem a prophecy of Ché's situation.

"Our brave and self-confident vanguard," Lenin explained, "was short of reserves in men and munitions, and there wasn't a single day when it had enough bread. It had to requisition bread and other food from the Polish peasants. That's why the Poles looked on the Red Army as enemies, not brothers and liberators."

So the constant flight through the regions of Caraparí, Yuque, and Ticucha was without reserves or bread. There was a battle at the Iquira mountain pass, where Ché lost matériel, one man, and a valuable collection of documents. These would soon be augmented by those turned up in four other caches, among them one from Ché's general headquarters at Ñancahuazú.

On September 22nd the documents were exhibited in Washington by the Bolivian ambassador, who denounced Guevara's presence in his country before a forum of Latin American ambassadors convened by the OAS. This had a strange effect: almost no one believed the photographs were really of Ché, either because they had been previously convinced of his death or because the Bolivian government's truthfulness was held in very low esteem.

And yet, during those same days, Guevara was falling back with a group of sixteen men before a force of fifteen hundred soldiers. The top military found the captured documents more convincing than the ambassadors had. They hadn't the slightest doubt: Ché was trapped. He was deep in a ravine matted with vegetation, but with heights that were completely barren, thus preventing him from getting out without being seen.

There was also the testimony of a guerrilla who, toward the end of September, gave himself up to the army, near the Rió Grande, taking refuge in the amnesty offered all those who surrendered immediately. He explained that Ché was seriously ill, but this appears to have been an exaggeration, at least at the time he made his report.

I returned to La Paz in September and obtained a permit to travel to Camiri, where I was present at the inauguration of the famous trial of Debray and Bustos, on the 26th. The guerrillas kept on the march. It was like a background chorus of armed men for the drama of this juridical travesty bringing together a thousand newsmen from all over the world and some of the most famous jurists of Europe and America. It was immediately plain that the trial was being used by the government as a formidable coercive wedge against the entire opposition within the country.

On that same day a battle took place at La Higuera, very near the Yuro ravine. It occurred in broad daylight, forcing the guerrillas to abandon their dead, three in all, one of them the Bolivian leader Roberto Peredo. They had just laid in a supply of rations and medicines when an army patrol appeared, and they had to fight.

From then on Ché's band broke up into smaller groups in order to move more freely. They reunited at night in previously arranged rendezvous. Guevara had to establish each area of operations in order to plan his route. He was busy with this on the 7th of October, when he realized he had completed eleven months of continued military operations in the jungle. He was optimistic about the future, as he wrote in his diary, reflecting that his guerrilla organization had developed "without complications" up to this time.

That day they had made contact with some peasants. An old woman tending a she-goat assured them she hadn't seen the soldiers for some time, but the guerrillas suspected she was lying. In the afternoon some of the men entered a house where there was another woman, with a daughter sick in bed. They left her some money to keep quiet, but had little hope that she would.

They resumed their march over some potato fiields beside irrigation ditches running out of the Yuro River. The ground registered their footprints.

On the 8th, a peasant woman notified the army that she had heard voices along the banks of the Yuro close to the spot where it ran into the San Antonio River. The military sent out several search patrols. Around 1:30 P.M., a burst of machine gun fire from the Rangers announced that contact with the guerrillas had been established.

The Bolivian miner, Simón Cuba, an excellent shot, was in the lead. He fired repeatedly, and quickly slipped out of sight. Behind him came Ché, who also fired until several bullets got him in the legs. In a heroic display of loyalty, Cuba picked up Ché and tried to carry him on his back out of the line of fire. But another volley wounded Ché again, knocking off his beret. Cuba then propped him up on the ground and decided to keep on shooting, although he was encircled at less than ten yards' distance. All the Rangers concentrated their fire on him. He died, riddled with bullets.

Ché was now in an impossible position, but he tried to put up a last stand. He leaned against a tree with one hand and operated his M2 with the other, even though it was a heavy, long weapon. He couldn't keep it up for more than a few minutes. He was wounded again in his right leg and another bullet hit the trigger of the M2. The gun jumped out of his hand, its stock split open, and the bullet went on to pierce his right forearm.

He was surrounded and taken prisoner.

He had several wounds, but his life wasn't in danger. Nor did he lose consciousness. He even saved the life of one of his pursuers, shot in the thigh and bleeding through his femoral artery, by ordering them to apply a tourniquet.

It was decided that the prisoner would be transferred to Higueras, about seven miles from the scene of the battle. From now on his fate depended on two men. One, Captain Gary Prado Salgado, commander of the Second Regiment of Rangers, was Ché's captor, and the other was Colonel Andrés Selnich, commander of the Third Tactical Group and Prado's military superior.

Prado was an army man educated in the United States. His father had been a general in the old army and one-time minister of war. He was an aristocrat, whom the enlisted men called "The English Gentleman." In his own way Selnich was also an aristocrat. In an army where nine out of ten men had Indian blood, Colonel Selnich's European origin was conspicuous and set him apart.

Guevara spoke to both. He was interested in knowing what units they belonged to, about their professional training, whether they had been at the counter-guerrilla school in Panama. His wounds were giving him trouble, and he was growing visibly weaker, although he was not hemorrhaging seriously. He couldn't move. They got ready to transfer him to La Higuera. Four soldiers carried him, stretched out on an army blanket, to a bare room in the town's schoolhouse and left him there.

During the next hours there was tense waiting among the officers and many comments and murmurs among the enlisted men. They knew that Major Niño de Guzmán wanted to take Guevara to Vallegrande, which he could reach in twenty minutes in the helicopter he piloted. It was even rumored that the Major quarreled with Colonel Selnich, who insisted on taking his wounded soldiers first.

There was a lot of deliberating between the captors and the military authorities, particularly Colonel Joaquín Zenteno Anaya, who was in charge of the army's Eighth Division and maintained telephone contact with La Paz. On the morning of October 9th the deliberations ended. Ché would be executed that same morning, at the place where he was being kept prisoner.

He was sitting on the floor, leaning his shoulder against the wall. He was weak and gasping for breath, and because the light was so poor, it took him a while to make out two persons entering the room.

Captain Prado came up behind Guevara and fired a burst from his machine gun at his neck, from above. Four bullets struck him. Colonel Selnich drew near and shot a single bullet from his 9-mm. pistol. It penetrated Ché's heart and one of his lungs. It was the coup de grâce. Ché's eyes were wide-open and very peaceful. There was a smile on his lips. He was dead.

photographs

Nine-year-old Ernesto Guevara exhibits a baseball glove. With him is his younger sister Celia.

Guevara (*front*), at ten, with brother and friends, visiting the Sierra de Cordoba, Argentina.

Celia de la Serna de Guevara, Ché's mother, leaves the Criminal Court House in Buenos Aires, where she was tried for political activities in 1964.

A 1950 advertisement by a motor-bicycle manufacturer, with a photograph of Ernesto Guevara and his letter praising their engine. Guevara was then twenty-two and had traveled through twelve Argentine provinces by motor-bike.

Facsimile of a short note Ché Guevara sent to his parents from
Sierra Maestra, to let them know that he was alive. It reads:
"Dear old ones: I am perfectly well. I have spent only two and
that leaves me five" (a reference to the seven lives of a cat).
"I am still working at the same thing. News is sporadic and will
continue to be so, but have faith that God is an Argentine" (a
popular expression). "A big hug for all. TETE" (the family's nickname for Guevara).

Ché Guevara and Ricardo Rojo (*Havana, 1961*).

Ricardo Rojo in Sierra de Escambray, Cuba, with the militia during military exercises against anti-Castrista guerrillas, a few weeks before the Bay of Pigs.

Lieutenant Eliseo de la Campa, Guevara's personal pilot, and Ricardo Rojo standing beside Guevara's twin-engine Cessna.

Rojo and Guevara, shaking hands, with Cuban cane cutters.

Photographs taken by Ricardo Rojo on the day of voluntary work described in Chapter 4. Shown are Ché; his wife, Aleida March; and the Argentine doctor, Alberto Granados, who accompanied Ché on his first trip out of Argentina and eventually came to live in Cuba.

Jorge Masetti, the Argentine journalist who commanded the guerrillas in Salta Province, Argentina, in 1964. (*Photographs were taken in Cuba in 1961.*)

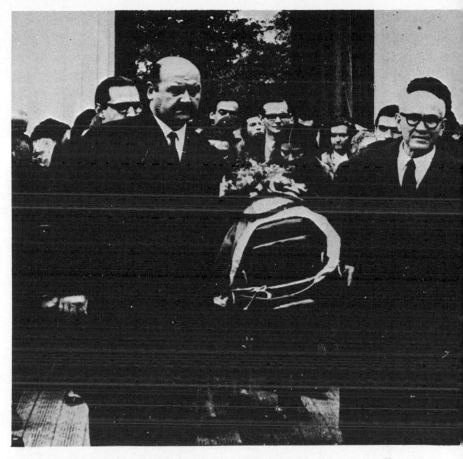

The burial of Ché's mother in May 1965; Ricardo Rojo is pall-bearer on left.

Guevara's farewell to his mother in April 1963 at the Havana airport.

Buenos Aires Abril 14 - 1965

Mi querido:

Mis cartas te suenan extrañas? No sé si hemos perdido la naturalidad con que nos hablábamos o si nunca la hemos tenido, y nos hemos hablado siempre en ese tono levemente irónico que practicamos los que vivimos a las dos orillas del Plata, agravado todavía por nuestro propio código familiar aún más cerrado.

El caso es que siempre una gran inquietud me ha hecho abandonar el tono irónico y ser directa. Parece que es entonces cuando mis cartas no se entienden y se vuelven extrañas y enigmáticas.

En este tono diplomático adoptado en nuestra correspondencia tengo yo también que leer entre líneas el significado oculto e interpretar. He leído tu última carta como leo las noticias publicadas en la Prensa o La Nación de Buenos Aires, desentrañando, o tratando de hacerlo, el verdadero significado de cada frase y el alcance de cada una.

El resultado ha sido un mar de confusiones y una intranquilidad y una alarma aún mayor.

No voy a usar lenguaje diplomático. Voy a ser muy directa. Me parece una verdadera locura que habiendo pocas cabezas con capacidad de organización en Cuba, todas ellas se vayan a cortar caña durante un mes, como ocupación principal, habiendo tantos y tan buenos macheteros entre el pueblo. Hacerlo como trabajo voluntario en tiempos normalmente dedicados al descanso o la distracción, un sábado o un Domingo, tiene otro sentido. También lo tiene hacerlo como trabajo principal cuando se trata de

demostrar de una manera concluyente, la ventaja y la necesidad del uso de las máquinas para el corte, cuando de la cosecha y del monto de toneladas de azúcar conseguida, saldrán las divisas con que contará Cuba.

Un mes es un largo período. Habrá para ello razones que ignoro.

Hablando ahora de tu caso personal, si después de ese mes te vas a dedicar a la dirección de una empresa, trabajo desempeñado con cierto éxito por Castellanos y Villegas, me parece que la locura alcanza el absurdo, sobre todo si este trabajo va a ser desempeñado durante 5 años para conseguir ser entonces un cuadro de verdad.

Como yo conocía tu empeño en no faltar ni un día de tu ministerio, cuando vi que tu viaje por el extranjero se prolongaba demasiado, mi pregunta era esta: ¿Seguirá siendo ministro de industrias cuando llegue a Cuba?, a quién se le ha dado la razón, o la primacía en la disputa por los motivos que deben de ser causales de la incentivación?

Las preguntas están contestadas a medias. Si te vas a dirigir una empresa es que has dejado de ser ministro. Depende de quién sea nombrado en tu lugar para saber si la disputa ha sido zanjada de un modo salomónico.

De todas maneras que te quedes 5 años dirigiendo una fábrica es un desperdicio demasiado grande para tu capacidad. Y no es la mamá la que está hablando. Es una vieja señora que aspira a ver el mundo entero convertido al socialismo. Creo que si haces lo que has dicho no vas a ser un buen servidor del socialismo mundial.

Si por cualquier razón los caminos se te han cerrado en Cuba, hay en Argelia un señor Ben Bella que te agradecería que le organizaras la economía allí o que lo asesoras

The last letter from Celia de la Serna de Guevara to her son (*see pages 173-175*).

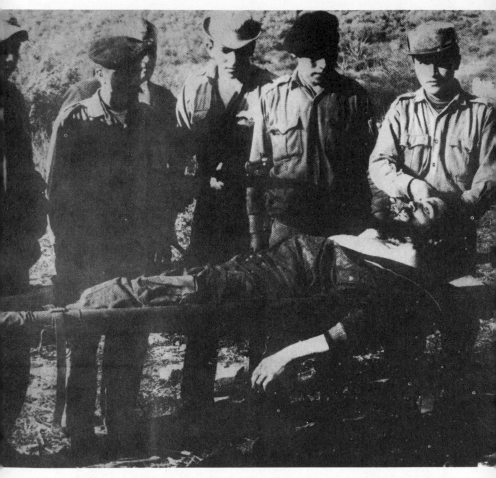

In Vallegrande, where he was taken by Bolivian soldiers and CIA agents (presumably Cubans), Ché's corpse is viewed by Bolivian Rangers.

Captain Gary Prado, commander of the Rangers who captured Ché. Despite accusations, he continues to deny that he killed Guevara. The military authorities nevertheless sent him to Rio de Janeiro, Brazil, for two years. Below, he describes to newsmen how Ché was captured.

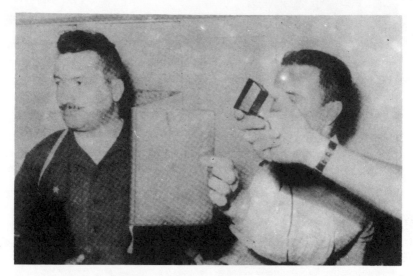

In Vallegrande, Colonel Joaquín Zenteno Anaya, commander of the Eighth Division of the Bolivian army, shows journalists the famous war diary seized from Ché.

Bolivian "Green Berets" eagerly read Ché's diary and try to find accounts of the battles in which they themselves took part. A contingent of 650 "Green Berets" was trained by Major Ralph Shelton, an American veteran of Laos and Vietnam.

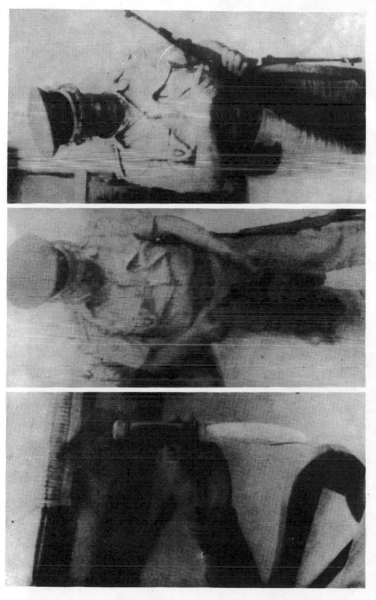

Colonel Zenteno Anaya exhibits Ché's equipment: a sturdy dagger for hand-to-hand combat, the knapsack in which the diary was found, and Ché's rifle. The Colonel points to the spot on the upper part of the rifle where a bullet hit, knocking it from his hand.

Bolivian doctors embalming Ché's body. A little later the Bolivian government announced that the body had been cremated.

Ché's body, shown from an angle which demonstrates very clearly the bullet's entrance below the left nipple. The bullet was shot upward from a low angle, and was identified as belonging to a caliber of gun (9 millimeter) reserved exclusively for Bolivian army officers.

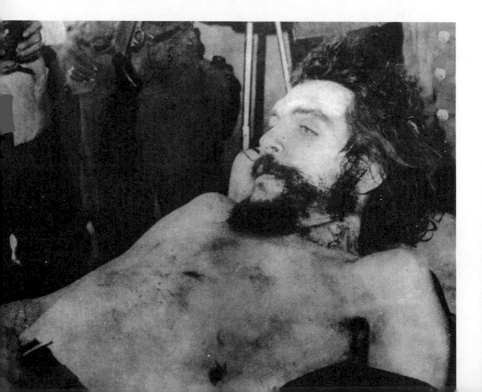

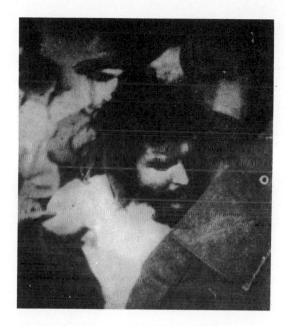

Ché's body being carried to Vallegrande by Bolivian soldiers. This photo and the one below help show how a popular cult of "Saint Ernesto of La Higuera" could have arisen among the peasants of the area in which he fought and died.

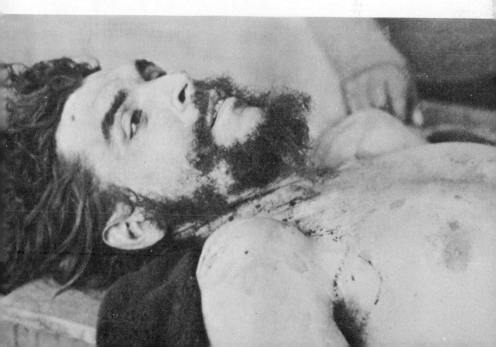

About the Author

Born in 1923 in Urdinarrain, Province Entre Ríos, Argentina, Ricardo Rojo was educated in Buenos Aires and received his law degree in 1949. He was, and still is, deeply involved in Latin American politics. Jailed by Peron, he was an early supporter of Arturo Frondizi and served in his administration from 1958 to 1960, as political adviser to the Argentine embassy in Bonn, Germany. In 1967, at a trial in Camiri, Bolivia, he represented the Argentine artist Ciro Bustos, co-defendant with French author-journalist Régis Debray; they had been arrested for their guerrilla activity with Ché Guevara. Mr. Rojo has published three books on law and Latin American politics and has been Professor of American History at the Colegio Libre de Mexico in Mexico City and an advisor in Economic Development at the Faculdad de Ciencias Economicas in Buenos Aires. He has traveled extensively throughout the world, and now makes his home in Buenos Aires with his wife, a psychologist and professor, and their two children.